JOHN
MURRAY
LEARNING

D1333703

WAY OF THE WOLF

Straight Line Selling:
Master the Art of Persuasion,
Influence, and Success

JORDAN BELFORT

JOHN
MURRAY
LEARNING

First published in the United States of America in 2017
by North Star Way, an imprint of Simon & Schuster, Inc.

This edition published in Great Britain in 2017 by John Murray Learning,
an imprint of Hodder & Stoughton. An Hachette UK company.

British Library Cataloguing in Publication Data: a catalogue
record for this title is available from the British Library.

Paperback: 978 1 4736 7481 3
eBook: 978 1 4736 7483 7
Audio book: 978 1 4736 7485 1

12

The publisher has used its best endeavours to ensure that any website addresses referred to in
this book are correct and active at the time of going to press. However, the publisher and the
author have no responsibility for the websites and can make no guarantee that a site will
remain live or that the content will remain relevant, decent or appropriate.

The publisher has made every effort to mark as such all words which it believes to be
trademarks. The publisher should also like to make it clear that the presence of a word in
the book, whether marked or unmarked, in no way affects its legal status as a trademark.

Every reasonable effort has been made by the publisher to trace the copyright holders of
material in this book. Any errors or omissions should be notified in writing to the
publisher, who will endeavour to rectify the situation for any reprints and future editions.

Printed and bound in Great Britain by CPI Group (UK) Ltd, Croydon, CR0 4YY.

John Murray Learning policy is to use papers that are natural, renewable
and recyclable products and made from wood grown in sustainable forests.
The logging and manufacturing processes are expected to conform
to the environmental regulations of the country of origin.

Carmelite House
50 Victoria Embankment
London EC4Y 0DZ

www.hodder.co.uk

It is tempting to dedicate this book to the person who has changed my life for the better and never stopped believing in me: my partner, Anne. But she has requested that I dedicate this book to the people all over the world who have come to my seminars, watched my videos, studied the Straight Line, written me for advice, and, most importantly, the ones who have written or gone out of their way to say "thank you." I have to acknowledge the fact that my life is mostly known for my crazy past. That is just one small part of it, and not the part that I am proud of or that I want to be remembered for. The people who have written to say that I give them the hope of second chances, that because I came back from massive failure they believe they too can overcome whatever situation they have found themselves in—to these people I dedicate this book. To the countless people who have written to tell me how the Straight Line System has changed their lives, their level of success, and their businesses in exponential ways—to you I dedicate this book. The creation of the Straight Line System changed my life forever. The skill sets it embodies have allowed me to recreate my life in ways even I never thought possible. I hope that this book will allow many more people to have access to the gift that keeps on giving. The Straight Line System truly is for everyone. My greatest close to date is that of my love, Anne. I hope that this book enables everyone who reads it to make their personal dreams come true too.

CONTENTS

PROLOGUE

THE BIRTH OF
A SALES SYSTEM

WHAT THEY SAY ABOUT ME IS TRUE.

I'm one of those natural *born* salesmen who can sell ice to an Eskimo, oil to an Arab, pork to a rabbi, or anything else you can think of.

But who really cares about that, right?

I mean, unless you want to hire me to sell one of your products, my ability to close is basically irrelevant to you.

Whatever the case, that's my gift: the ability to sell anything to anyone, in massive quantities; and whether this gift comes from God or from nature, I really can't say, although what I *am* able to say—with absolute certainty, in fact—is that I am not the only person who was born with it.

There are a handful of others who are *sort of* like me.

The reason they are only *sort of* like me has to do with another precious gift I possess, a gift that's infinitely more rare and infinitely more valuable, and that offers a massive benefit to everyone. *Including you.*

What is this amazing gift?

Quite simply, it's the ability to take people from all walks of life regardless of age, race, creed, color, socioeconomic background, educational status, and level of natural sales ability, and turn that person into a world-class closer almost instantly.

It's a bold statement, I know, but let me put it to you this way: if I were a superhero, then training salespeople would be my superpower, and there's not a soul on the planet who does it better than me.

Now, that sounded totally awful, right?

I can only imagine what you're thinking right now.

"What a cocky bastard this guy is! So conceited! So damn full of himself! Let's throw the bastard to the wolves!

"Oh, *wait!* He already *is* a wolf, isn't he?"

Actually, I'm an erstwhile wolf. But, either way, I think it's time to formally introduce myself.

I'm the Wolf of Wall Street. *Remember me?* The one who Leonardo DiCaprio played on the silver screen, the one who took thousands of young kids, who could barely walk and chew gum at the same time, and turned them into world-class closers using a seemingly magical sales training system called the Straight Line? The one who tortured all those panic-stricken New Zealanders at the end of the movie because they couldn't sell me a pen the right way? You remember.

On the heels of Black Monday, I took control of an irrelevant little brokerage firm named Stratton Oakmont and moved it out to Long Island to seek my fortune, and it was there, in the spring of 1988, that I cracked the code for human influence and developed that seemingly magical system for training salespeople.

Its name was the Straight Line System—or the Straight Line, for short—a system that proved to be so powerful and effective, and so easy to learn, that within days of inventing it, it brought massive wealth and success to anyone I taught it to. In consequence, thousands of young men and women began pouring into Stratton's boardroom, looking to hop on the Straight Line gravy train and stake their claim in the American Dream.

For the most part, they were a decidedly *average* lot at best—basically the sad, forgotten spawn of America's working-class families.

They were kids who had never been told by their parents that they were capable of greatness; any greatness that they naturally had in them had been literally conditioned out of them since the day they were born. By the time they made it into my boardroom, they were trying merely to survive, not to thrive.

But in a post–Straight Line world, none of that mattered anymore. Things like education and intellect and natural sales ability were mere trivialities that could be easily overcome. All you had to do was show up at my door, promise to work your ass off, and I would teach you the Straight Line System and make you rich.

But, alas, there was also a dark side to all this precocious success. You see, the system turned out to be almost *too* effective. It created freshly minted millionaires at such a ferocious clip that they ended up skipping over the typical life struggles that most young men and women go through that serve to build their characters. The result was success without respect, wealth without restraint, and power without responsibility—and, *just like that*, things began to spiral out of control.

And so it was that, in the same way that a seemingly innocuous tropical storm uses the warm waters of the Atlantic to grow and build and strengthen and mutate until it reaches a point of such critical mass that it destroys everything in its path, the Straight Line System followed an eerily similar trajectory—destroying everything in its path as well, including me.

Indeed, by the time it was over I had lost everything: my money, my pride, my dignity, my self-respect, my children—for a time—and my freedom.

But the worst part of all was that I knew I had no one to blame but myself. I had taken a God-given gift and misused it, and I had taken an amazing discovery and bastardized it.

The Straight Line System had the ability to change people's lives in a dramatic way—leveling the playing field for anyone who'd been held back from achieving greatness due to an inability to effectively communicate their thoughts and ideas in a way that connected with other people and moved them to take action.

And what did I do with it?

Well, besides breaking a fair number of records for the consumption of dangerous recreational drugs, I used my discovery of the world's most powerful sales training system to live out every adolescent fantasy I'd ever had, while empowering thousands of others to do the same.

So, yes, I deserved exactly what I got: completely wiped out.

But, of course, the story doesn't end there; and how could it, after all? I mean, how could a system that created such massive wealth and success for anyone who learned it simply fade away into obscurity?

It couldn't. And, of course, it didn't.

It started with the thousands of ex-Strattonites who, after leaving the firm, began spreading the system around—bringing a watered-down version of it to a dozen different industries. Yet, no matter where they went or how watered down the version was, learning even a *fraction* of the Straight Line System was enough to take a struggling salesperson and turn them into a solid producer.

Then *I* got involved.

On the heels of two bestselling memoirs and a blockbuster Scorsese movie, I spread an undiluted version across the entire world, to virtually every business and industry. From banking to brokerage to telco to the auto industry to real estate to insurance to financial planning, to plumbers to doctors to lawyers to dentists to online marketers to offline marketers—and basically everyone in between. As amazing as the results had been the *last* time around, *this* time they were even better.

You see, before I began teaching the system again, I spent two full years going line by line through its code—taking every last *nuance* and pushing it to an even higher level of operational proficiency, while ensuring that every last bit was grounded at the highest level of ethics and integrity.

Gone were any high-pressure sales tactics, questionable language patterns, or even the slightest reference to closing a sale at all costs to simply earn a commission; all of these were *purged* from the system in favor of more elegant strategies. It was a painstaking process, where no expense was spared and no stone left unturned.

World-class experts were brought in to review every aspect of the system—from occupational psychologists to experts in content creation, best adult-learning practices, and neuro-linguistic programming. And what emerged in its place was something truly incredible: a system that was so powerful and effective, and that maintained such a high level of ethics and integrity, that I knew in my heart that the Straight Line System had finally evolved into what I always knew it could be:

A money-making force for good.

What I offer you on the following pages is a turnkey solution for applying the Straight Line System to any business or industry.

For those of you in sales, or if you own your own business, this book will be a total game-changer for you. It will show you how to shorten your sales cycle, increase your closing rate, develop a steady stream of customer referrals, and create customers for life. In addition, it will also offer you a paint-by-number formula for building and maintaining a world-class sales force.

And, for those of you who are *not* in sales, this book will be equally as valuable to you. You see, one of the costliest mistakes that "civilians" make is that they tend to think of sales and persuasion in traditional terms only, where there's a salesperson closing a deal. So, they ask themselves, "Since I'm not in sales, what's the point of learning how to sell?"

Meanwhile, nothing could be further from the truth.

Even if you're not in "sales," you still need to become at least *reasonably proficient* at sales and persuasion. Otherwise, you're going to find yourself living a *severely* disempowered life.

Selling is *everything* in life.

In fact, either you're selling or you're failing.

You're selling people that your ideas make sense, your concepts make sense, your products make sense: you could be a parent selling your kids on the importance of taking a bath or doing their homework; you could be a teacher selling your students on the value of education; a lawyer selling a jury on the innocence of your client; a pastor selling your congregation on the existence of God or Jesus of Mohammad or Buddha; a politician selling your constituency on the benefits of voting for a certain referendum—in short, selling applies to *all* people, and *all* aspects of life, both business and personal. After all, at some point in our lives, we'll all have to sell ourselves to someone: a prospective partner, a future employer, a future *employee*, a future first date, and on and on.

Then you have all the day-to-day business scenarios that fall outside of what we normally consider *sales*—an entrepreneur trying to raise venture capital or secure a line of credit at a bank; selling your employees, or someone you're courting to become an employee, on the power and righteousness of your vision for the future; negotiating a new lease for office space; securing a better interest rate on your merchant account or negotiating better payment terms with a vendor.

Again, it doesn't matter what line of work you're in or if it's business or personal. We're *always* trying to convey our thoughts and ideas and hopes and dreams in a way that not only moves people to take action but that also gets us what we want in life too.

That's what *ethical persuasion* is all about; and without that one, linchpin skill, it is very difficult to achieve success, at any reasonable level, or live an empowered life.

In fact, at the end of the day, that's what this book is really all about. By providing you with a simple, proven way to master the art of communication, you'll be able to move through life with far greater personal power and live a far more empowered life.

Just always remember the words of Spider-Man's uncle, from the first *Spider-Man* movie. "With great power," he warned, "comes great responsibility."

This book will grant you that power.

I urge you to please use it responsibly.

1

CRACKING THE CODE FOR SALES AND INFLUENCE

"DON'T YOU GUYS GET IT? EVERY SALE IS THE SAME!"

The first time I uttered those words to a roomful of salesmen was on a Tuesday evening, in 1988, and what I got in return were some very confused looks. They were looks that so much as said, "What the hell are you talking about, Jordan? Every sale is *not* the same! Every sale is *different*. Our prospects all have different needs, different beliefs, different values, different objections, and different pain points. So how could every sale possibly be the same?"

In retrospect, I can see their point.

In fact, I can see *all* their points—the points of the millions upon millions of people who have attended my Straight Line seminars all over the world, and who have cocked their heads to the side and narrowed their eyes skeptically when I got up onstage and said, with absolute certainty, that *every sale is the same*.

After all, it *seems* like a rather far-fetched notion, doesn't it?

I mean, even if you put aside the obvious points that I listed above, how could every sale possibly be the same? Take the countless number of goods and services for sale in the global marketplace: they too are all different. Take the personal financial situations of your prospects:

they're all different too. And take the unique sets of preconceived notions that each prospect brings with them into the sale—not just about your product but also about you, about trusting salespeople in general, and about the decision-making process itself as it relates to buying. Again, they're all different.

Indeed, when you take all the *apparent* differences that can pop up in a sale at any time, it comes as no surprise that only a tiny percentage of the population feels comfortable at the thought of entering a situation that requires sales and influence. The rest of the world actively shies away from it—despite knowing how absolutely *crucial* it is to the achievement of wealth and success.

Even *worse*, among those very select few who *do* feel comfortable, only a tiny percentage of them will ever attain the status of being a top producer. The rest will plod along somewhere in the middle, stuck in the muck and mire of mediocrity and averagism. They'll earn *just* enough to keep "selling" worthwhile (after all, even a decent salesperson will make more money closing sales than in a non–sales related job), but they'll never experience the financial freedom of being a top producer. It will always remain *just* out of reach.

It's a sad reality, for sure, but such is the plight of any salesperson who believes that every sale is different—a discovery that hit me like an atomic bomb and led directly to the creation of the Straight Line System.

My discovery didn't come about slowly. It came all at once, during an emergency sales training session I held in Stratton's original boardroom. At the time, I had only twelve brokers working for me, and, at this particular moment—precisely 7:15 p.m. on that very Tuesday evening—they were sitting directly across from me and wearing those confused, skeptical expressions that I would come to know so well.

As the story goes, exactly four weeks prior to that, I had stumbled upon an untapped niche in the retail stock market, which was selling five-dollar stocks to the richest 1 percent of Americans. For whatever reason, no one on Wall Street had ever tried it before; and when I tested the idea myself, the results were *so* incredible that I decided to completely reinvent the firm.

At the time, Stratton was selling penny stocks to average moms-and-pops, and we were having *massive* success since the day the firm opened. In fact, by the end of our third month, the average broker—or *Strattonite*, as they liked to call themselves—was already earning more than $12,000 in monthly commission, and one of them was earning more than triple that.

That broker was none other than Danny Porush, my future junior partner, who would end up being immortalized on the silver screen by a slimmed down, buck-toothed version of Jonah Hill, who loosely portrayed him in the movie *The Wolf of Wall Street*.

Whatever the case, Danny was the first person I'd ever taught how to sell penny stocks, and as luck would have it, he turned out to be a *born* salesperson, like me. At the time, we both worked at a small penny stock firm called the Investor Center, and Danny was my assistant. When I left to open Stratton, I brought Danny with me and he'd been my right-hand man ever since.

In fact, it was Danny who wrote that first massive buy ticket with a wealthy investor, on the fifth day of the test. His commission on this one single trade was *$72,000*, an amount so incomprehensibly large that if I hadn't seen it for myself, I wouldn't have believed it. To give you some perspective, it was over a *hundred times* greater than the average commission on a penny stock trade. It was nothing short of a total game-changer.

To this very day, I'll never forget the look on Danny's face when he walked into my office holding that golden buy ticket; and I'll *also* never forget looking out into the boardroom myself, a few moments later, after I'd regained my composure, and seeing my entire future unfold right before my eyes. In that very instant, I knew that this would be the last day that Stratton ever sold penny stocks to *anyone*. What with the massive financial firepower that a wealthy investor could bring to bear, it simply didn't make sense to cold-call average moms-and-pops ever again. It was as simple as that.

All that was left to do was to teach the Strattonites how to close rich people, and the rest, as they say, would be history.

————————————

Unfortunately, as they *also* say, "Easier said than done!"

As it turned out, training a bunch of barely post-adolescent nincompoops to go toe-to-toe with America's wealthiest investors was far more challenging than I could have ever possibly anticipated. In fact, it turned out to be totally fucking impossible.

After four weeks of cold-calling, the Strattonites hadn't closed a single new account. Not even *one*! Even worse, because it was my idea to make the switch, the brokers were holding me personally responsible for their current state of misery.

In essence, they had gone from earning $12,000 a month to making zero dollars a month, and I had run out of ideas on how to train them. And make no mistake: I had tried *everything*.

After failing miserably with my *own* system, I read through countless books on sales, listened to tapes, attended local seminars; I even flew clear across the country to Los Angeles, California, to attend a three-day sales seminar that was purported to have the world's greatest sales trainers all under one roof.

But, again, I came up empty-handed.

Disturbing as it was, after one full month of intelligence gathering, the most valuable piece of intelligence that I'd been able to gather was that my *own* system of training was far more advanced than anything else out there; and if *that* wasn't cutting it, where was I to go from there? I was starting to think that maybe it was just impossible.

Perhaps the Strattonites were simply constitutionally incapable of closing rich people. They were too young and too uneducated to be taken seriously by them. Yet how would that explain the massive success that Danny and I were still having as we continued to dial through our leads? My personal closing rate had climbed to over 50 percent by now, and Danny's was in the low thirties.

How could we all be dialing through the same leads, using the same script, pitching the same stock, and yet getting such dramatically different results? It was enough to make a person insane; or, even *worse*, to make them jump ship.

By the end of week four, the Strattonites had basically given up. They were desperate to go back to the world of penny stocks and were teetering on the edge of mutiny.

So there I was, at the front of the boardroom, desperate for a breakthrough. What I was about to realize, however, was that I'd actually just made one.

Looking back at that moment now, standing before the brokers and trying to explain how every sale is the same, I would have never guessed how close I was to inventing the world's most powerful sales training system.

You see, when I said that every sale is the same, what I meant that night, and what turned out to be one of the most profound ideas

I've ever had, is that despite all those aforementioned differences—individual needs, objections, values, pain points—despite all that *stuff*, the same three key elements must still line up in any prospect's mind before you have a shot at closing them.

Let me repeat that: the reason every sale is the same is because, despite all that individual *stuff*, the same three key elements still have to line up in any prospect's mind before you have a shot at closing them.

And it doesn't matter what you're selling or how you're selling it; how much it costs or how much money the prospect has; and whether it's tangible or intangible, over the phone or in person. If in a single moment in time, you can create these three crucial elements in a prospect's mind, then you've got an excellent shot of closing. Conversely, if even one of them is *missing*, you have basically no shot at all.

The Three Tens

We call these three core elements the Three Tens—with the context being a prospect's current state of certainty on a scale from one to ten.

For example, if a prospect is currently at a "ten" on the certainty scale, then it means he or she is in a state of *absolute certainty* at that moment. Conversely, if the prospect's currently at a "one," then they are in a state of absolute *uncertainty* at that moment.

Now, in sales, when we talk about *certainty*, the first thing that pops into people's minds is certainty about the actual *product* being sold. In other words, before there's any chance of a prospect buying a product, they first have to be *absolutely* certain that the product makes sense to them, insofar as it filling their needs, eliminating *any* pain they might have, being a good value for the money . . . and so forth.

So—the first of the Three Tens is your *product*.

THE THREE TENS

1 **The product, idea, or concept**

2

3

In essence, your prospect must be absolutely certain that they *love* your product, or as we like to say with the Straight Line System, your prospect must think it's the best thing since sliced bread!

This includes both *tangible* products like cars, boats, houses, food, clothing, consumer products, and all the various services people perform; and also *intangible* products, like ideas and concepts and values and beliefs, or any vision you might have for the future.

Over the years, I've found that the simplest and most effective way to explain the Three Tens is to imagine a "continuum of certainty," like the one below.

Uncertainty

1 ———————————— 10

Absolute   **Absolute**
Uncertainty   **Certainty**

Now, notice how on the very *right* end of the continuum, you have the number 10. This represents your prospect being in a state of absolute *certainty* about the value and efficacy of your product, or put more simply, your prospect absolutely *loves* it!

For example, if you were to ask this prospect what they thought about your product, a dead-honest answer would sound something like: "Oh my god, it's literally the *best* thing since sliced bread! Not only does it fill all my needs but it's also a great value for the money! I can only imagine how great I'm going to feel when I get to use it in the future. It'll be like having a huge weight lifted off my shoulders!"

That's a *10* on the certainty scale: your prospect absolutely *loves* your product, and they're damn sure of it.

Then, over on the very *left* end of the continuum, you have the number 1. This represents your prospect being in a state of absolute *uncertainty* about the value and efficacy of your product, or put more simply, they think it's a total piece of shit.

In this case, if you were to ask your prospect the *same* question as above, they would say something along the lines of: "That product of yours is the biggest piece of shit I've seen in my life! In fact, not only is it completely overpriced, but it also looks like shit, works like shit, feels like shit, and it's actually built like shit. So the sooner you get that piece of shit out of my sight, the happier I'll be."

That's a *1* on the certainty scale: your prospect absolutely *despises* your product, and it's going to be difficult to change their mind.

Then, along the continuum's middle, you have the varying degrees of certainty between a 1 and a 10, with the number 5 representing a state of pure ambivalence. That's where your prospect isn't leaning one way or the other. In normal sales parlance, this is referred to as your prospect "sitting on the fence," an expression specifically meant to highlight the delicate nature of this state. However, with the Straight Line System, we view a 5 in a far more positive light. In fact, to a seasoned Straight Liner, a prospect who is at a 5 has a big sign on their chest, saying:

PLEASE INFLUENCE ME NOW!
I CAN'T MAKE UP MY MIND,
SO PLEASE HELP ME!

The important thing to remember here is that, while being at a 5 does, indeed, mean that your prospect is fifty-fifty on your product, it does *not* mean that you only have a fifty-fifty chance of closing them.

The same thing goes for levels 3 and 7 on the certainty scale, which are basically mirror images of each other. In the case of a 3, your prospect thinks that your product is basically *crap*, although not nearly as crappy as if they were at a 1. And at a 7, your prospect thinks your product is great, although not *nearly* as great as if they were at a 10.

In both of these cases, however, whether your prospect is at a 7 or a 3, there are two important things to remember. First, your prospect's feelings of certainty or uncertainty are less set in stone than if they were at the level to the right or the left of them. Secondly, their presence at either level does not directly translate into a better or worse chance of ultimately closing them. In other words, their current state of certainty is just that—*current*. It is not permanent, and they are eagerly waiting to be influenced by you.

Now, when it comes time to ask for the order, it doesn't take a rocket scientist to figure out that the closer you've gotten your prospect to a 10, the better chance you have of closing them. On the other hand, the farther away your prospect is from a 10, the worse chance you have of closing them. From a practical standpoint, if your prospect is anywhere below a 5, you have basically no chance of closing them. The reason for this has to do with something called *positive intent*, which serves as the very foundation from which all human beings make their decisions.

In other words, human beings don't buy things that they think will make their lives *worse*; they buy things that they think will make their lives better. However, the operative word here is *think*. You see, just because someone has positive intent doesn't necessarily mean that the resulting decisions will end up having a positive impact on them.

In fact, with many people, it often doesn't. Their lives are punctuated by a series of self-defeating decisions. However, even these "serial bad decision-makers" *believe* their decisions were good when they made them. That's the definition of positive intent.

In consequence, when you ask for the order, if your prospect thinks that your product is *shit* then you have absolutely no chance of closing them. Conversely, if they think the *opposite* is true—that your product is the *best thing since sliced bread*—then you have an excellent chance of closing them.

It's basic logic, right?

So, let me ask you this:

Let's say you've just made an absolutely *kick-ass* sales presentation to a financially qualified prospect who needs your product, wants your product, and who's also been feeling a bit of *pain* as a result of an unfulfilled need that your product perfectly meets. In addition, let's *also* say that your sales presentation was so "on target" that when you asked your prospect for the order, they were at a 10 on the certainty scale, and *damn* sure of it. My question is, will the prospect buy from you, yes or no?

The obvious answer is *yes*, isn't it?

Before you answer the question, I want you to know that I've laid out this same scenario to audiences all over the world and posed that very same question. When I ask the people in the audience to raise their hands if they think a prospect will buy from them under those circumstances, every hand in the room goes flying up.

It doesn't matter where I am in the world, how large the audience is, or how much sales experience they have. Unless they've been taught the Straight Line System, their hands always go up.

And that's when I deliver the punch line.

I say, "*Really?* Well, guess what? You're all wrong. The correct answer is *maybe*. Maybe they will, and maybe they won't." You see, I was purposely being a bit coy with you before, and I left out one crucial point from that scenario I laid out.

What if the prospect doesn't trust you?

For instance, let's say that, during your sales presentation, you accidentally said something or did something that rubbed the prospect the wrong way, to the point where they no longer trusted you. What are the chances of them buying from you then?

I'll tell you what they are: *Zero! Nothing! Zilch!*

Plain and simple, if your prospect doesn't trust you, then there's absolutely no way they are going to buy from you. And, again, I don't care *how* certain they are about your product; they still won't buy from you. In fact, if they're *that* intent on purchasing your product, then they simply find someone else who sells the same thing—a salesperson they *trust*—and they will buy it from that salesperson instead. It's as simple as that.

So, that's what makes up the *second* of the Three Tens:

You!

THE THREE TENS

1 **The product, idea, or concept**

2 **You, trust and connect with you**

3

For example, do they think you're a likable, trustworthy person, who is not only an expert in your field but also prides yourself on putting your customer's needs first and making sure that if any problems arise you'll be right there on the spot to resolve them?

That would be a *10* on the certainty scale.

Or do they think you're an unlikable "snake in the grass," a stone-cold novice who'll stick the knife in their back the moment they turn it from you, because all you care about is extracting the maximum amount of commission out of the deal and then moving on to the next target as quickly as possible?

That would be a *1* on the certainty scale.

And in between those two extremes you have all the varying degrees of certainty as you move up and down the scale.

For example, maybe the prospect thinks you're *reasonably* trust-worthy, but they just don't *like* you very much. Maybe you broke rap-port with them as a result of something you said during your sales presentation—or perhaps it happened even *earlier* than that, at the moment the prospect first laid eyes on you. Maybe there was something about the way you looked, or the way you shook their hand, or how much eye contact you made, that turned the prospect off and, hence, stopped you from falling into a deep state of rapport with them.

Or maybe it was the way you asked questions when you were trying to gather intelligence, to identify their needs and values and to see if they were financially qualified. Perhaps you came off as the "Grand Inquisitor" type—asking questions with the sort of laser-guided focus that makes people feel like you care more about maximizing your com-mission than resolving their pain.

Whatever the case, my point is that, in the same way that you have varying degrees of certainty for how the prospect feels about your product, there are also varying degrees of certainty for how the prospect feels about *you*.

In consequence, if you want your prospect to say yes when you ask for the order, then you're going to need to have them as close to a 10 as possible for *both* of those things: you *and* your product.

Now let me ask you this:

Let's say that you're able to get your prospect to a level *very* close to a 10 for both things. Will they buy from you then, yes or no?

Hopefully, you've caught on by now, and you've figured out that the answer will be the same as last time, which was *maybe*—as in: maybe they will, and maybe they won't.

You see, like last time, I left out one very crucial point from the scenario—namely: *What if your prospect doesn't trust the company you work for?*

For example, let's say your prospect read something very negative about your company, something that led them to believe that the company might not stand behind the product you're offering or that they would get poor customer service if any problems arose. What are the chances of them buying from you under that circumstance?

They're slim and nil; and slim, as they say, left town.

It's really quite simple: if your prospect doesn't trust the company you work for, then there's absolutely no way they are going to buy from you—so long as you continue to work there, or until you can convince them otherwise.

And, again, I don't care *how* certain they are about the first two Tens. They will simply not buy from you if they think the company you work for will ultimately try to screw them.

So that's what makes up the *third* of the Three Tens.

THE THREE TENS

1 **The product, idea, or concept**

2 **You, trust and connect with you**

3 **The prospect must trust and connect with the company**

In fact, this is why it's so much easier to sell to existing customers than to new ones, *even* if you don't have a personal relationship with them. The fact that they have an existing relationship with your *company* means that the third Ten has already been established, leaving you with only the first and the second Tens to address.

Now, if you work for a Fortune 500 company with an impeccable reputation, then the chances are extremely high that your prospect will walk into the sale *already* at a very high level of certainty for the third Ten. That's plainly obvious, right?

However, what's *not* quite as obvious is that in addition to having the third Ten established, there's also an extremely high likelihood that your prospect will walk into the sale feeling a very high level of certainty for the first and second Tens as well!

In other words, before you even open your mouth, the prospect is *also* going to be inclined to trust *you* (because reputable companies choose their employees carefully and take the time to train them) and the product you're offering (because reputable companies have too much to lose selling low-quality products).

Conversely, if you're working for a company that has a *questionable* reputation, then your prospects are going to enter the sales encounter at *far* lower levels of certainty; in fact, depending on how bad that reputation is, you can find yourself fighting a serious uphill battle with your prospects, as many of them will be entering the sales encounter with a certainty level below 3.

Lastly, if you're working for a small company whose reputation is neither good nor bad, but simply unknown, that will have little impact on where your prospect enters the encounter on the certainty scale, other than the usual skepticism that's created by dealing with a company that you've never heard of before.

Whichever the case, the most important thing to remember is that your prospect will always enter the sales encounter at *some* point on the certainty scale. Just where, who really knows? After all, we're not mind readers. However, what we *do* know is that your prospect will definitely be *somewhere* on the scale, because they haven't just arrived from outer space or crawled out from under a rock. Your prospect has been living right here, on planet Earth, which means that they will have had at least *some* type of experience with the type of product you're selling and the industry you're in.

For example, let's say you're a car salesman, working in a Mercedes dealership. Even if your prospect has never driven or even *sat* in a Mercedes before, you wouldn't expect them to react like one of those shrieking chimpanzees in *2001: A Space Odyssey* and start jumping up and down on the hood, as if trying to make sense of some completely foreign object.

Get the picture?

My point here is that, no matter what product you're selling, whether your prospect walks in your door or answers your cold call or clicks on your website, they will always enter the encounter with a preconceived notion about you, about your product, and about the company you work for.

You see, we all arrive at any particular moment in time with a history of beliefs and values and opinions and experiences and victories and defeats and insecurities and decision-making strategies—and then based on all of that *stuff*, our brain, working at near light speed, will instantly relate it to whatever scenario lies before it. Then, based on the result, it will place us at whatever point on the certainty scale it deems appropriate for each of the Three Tens—and it's from that starting point that we can then be influenced.

Now, if you think that sounds a bit complicated, have no fear: I promise you that it's not. In fact, once you become even *reasonably* proficient with the Straight Line System, you'll be able to take any prospect, regardless of *where* they started off on the certainty scale, and move them to higher and higher levels of certainty with remarkable ease. It will simply be a matter of taking immediate control of the sale, and then moving your prospect, step by step, down the straight line, from the open to the close, and building massive certainty along the way.

Two Types of Certainty

Before we move forward, there's just one more thing about certainty that I need to fill you in on—namely, that there are actually two types of it: you have logical certainty, and you have emotional certainty, and they're entirely different things.

LOGICAL CERTAINTY

Logical certainty is based primarily on the words you say. For instance, does the case you've made to the prospect add up on an intellectual level? I'm talking about the actual facts and figures, the features and benefits, and the long-term value proposition, as it relates specifically to that prospect.

In other words, from a sober, emotionless perspective, does the idea or *thesis* that you've presented to them make sense? Does your product or service truly fill their needs? Is it priced fairly when compared to the competition? Does the cost-benefit ratio make it an unequivocally great deal?

When a prospect is feeling logically certain about your product, they can go from start to finish and connect all the dots in the logical case you've made without finding any holes in your story. As a result, they feel confident in their ability to tell the story to someone else and, if necessary, convince *that* person that they are 100 percent justified to feel the way they do—that, from a purely empirical perspective, the truth is on the their side.

That's what logical certainty is all about.

EMOTIONAL CERTAINTY

On the flip side, emotional certainty is based on a gut feeling that something *must* be good. Once it hits us, we feel a *craving* inside that simply must be fulfilled, even if there's a heavy price to pay for fulfilling it.

Unlike logical certainty, *emotional* certainty has to do with painting your prospect a picture of the future where they've bought your product and can see themselves using the product and feeling good as a result of it.

We call this technique *future pacing*, and it serves as the very backbone of how we move someone emotionally.

When you future pace someone, you're essentially playing out the post-buying movie in the best fashion possible—allowing that person to experience your product's amazing benefits *right now*, along with the positive feelings they create. The prospect's needs have been filled; their pain has been resolved; any itch the they had has been scratched, and they are feeling wonderful as a result of it.

Now, if you're wondering which of the two kinds of certainty is more important, the answer is they're *both* important—and they're both absolutely crucial if you want to close at the highest level.

You see, people don't buy on logic; they buy on emotion, and then justify their *decision* with logic. The logical mind is analytical by nature, so the more information you give it the more information it wants to know. In consequence, if you get your prospect to a high level of logical certainty, they'll say, "It sounds great, let me think about it . . ." or "Let me do a bit more research and I'll call you back."

However, if you skip making the logical case and focus strictly on creating emotional certainty, it won't do the trick either, because the logical mind serves as a human bullshit detector. It stops us from being swept away by our emotions if things don't add up logically. In consequence, if you want to close at the highest level, then you're going to have to create *both* types of certainty—logical and emotional—which is precisely what you'll be doing as you move your prospect down the straight line, from the open to the close. (More on this later—*lots* more!)

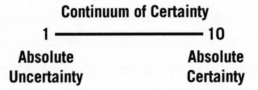

So let me sum things up for you, one last time, before we take the next step forward.

Plain and simple, if you've been able to move your prospect to a very high level of certainty (both types of certainty!) for each of the Three Tens, then you have an excellent shot of closing them. Conversely, if even one of the Three Tens has *not* been lined up, then you have *no shot* of closing them at all.

However, to be clear, when I say *no shot*, I don't mean that the prospect will hit you with an outright *no*. In fact, when you're following the principles of the Straight Line System, you will almost never hear the *word* no, except at the very beginning of the sale, when you're first introducing yourself or when you're *qualifying* the prospect.

At those points in the sale, you *will* hear the word no; and that's absolutely fine. In fact, it's an important aspect of the Straight Line System, as one of its cornerstone philosophies is that we do not make a full-blown sales presentation to someone who is not interested in buying what we're selling.

Instead, we want to weed these people out as quickly as possible, during the intelligence-gathering phase. (More on that later.) Remember, it's not the job of salespeople to turn nos into yeses; it's simply not what they do. Instead, we turn "Let me think about it" into a yes, and "Let me call you back" into a yes, and "I need to speak to my wife" into a yes, and "It's a bad time of year" into a yes.

In traditional sales parlance, we refer to these various *statements* as "objections," and they come up mostly in the back end of the sale, after you've asked for the order for the first time.

In reality, though, the actual *meaning* of any particular objection has very little to do with what it states on the surface.

You see, at the end of the day, objections are merely smoke screens for uncertainty for one or all of the Three Tens.

In other words, if you ask for the order and your prospect is not high enough on the certainty scale, then they'll throw out a smoke screen in the form of one of the common objections, as opposed to coming clean with you, which would mean revealing specifically which of the Three Tens was holding them back.

Now, there *are* some exceptions to this, which I'll get to a bit later, but my point is that, more than 95 percent of the time, the common objections are merely ploys on the part of the prospect, who would rather bow out of the sale gracefully than have to look the salesperson in the eye and confront them about their lack of certainty concerning the Three Tens.

For example, it's far less confrontational to say, "Let me think about it" or "It's a bad time of year," to someone who's just spent the last ten minutes telling you how wonderful a product is than to say, "I don't trust you" or "I think your product stinks" or "I don't like your company" or "I can't afford it right now" or "Your product seems kind of great, but I'm not *1000 percent* sure of that, and I simply can't afford to risk being wrong and have my spouse chasing me around the house screaming: 'I told you so! I told you so!'"

So, to avoid the possibility of a head-on confrontation, the prospect conjures up a little white lie, a *special* lie, a lie that gives the salesperson *just enough* false hope to make them think that there is a shot of getting a callback by ending the encounter now, without pressing the prospect any further.

To that end, the prospect will often start off their objection with a quick one-liner about how much they like your product.

For example, the prospect might start with something like, "It sounds pretty good, Jim," or "It seems really interesting, Jim," and then follow it up with, "I just need to speak to my wife first. How about I give you a call back tomorrow?"

And, with that, the prospect has set themself up to gracefully bow out of the sale, while the salesperson, if they were naïve enough to buy into this charade, has not only eliminated any chance of closing the deal but has also been set up for massive pain when they start dialing through the list of callbacks, which consists of people who had no intention of buying in the first place.

Before we move on, I just want to dispel any notion you might have that Straight Line's strategy for handling objections is going to promote, support, or even *remotely recommend* the use of high-pressure sales tactics in any way whatsoever.

Simply put, it *won't*.

See, what I was talking about before was something entirely different—namely, that it serves *both* the prospect *and* the salesperson to be honest and forthright with each other during a sales encounter, and that anything else is a complete waste of time.

With the Straight Line System, we don't leave a crucial outcome like *honest communication* up to chance. We *ensure* it by making it the sole responsibility of the salesperson, and then providing him or her with a bulletproof formula to achieve that outcome every time.

So, with that, let's go back to that very Tuesday evening, when the idea for the Straight Line System came bubbling into my brain. Coincidentally, it was the subject of handling objections that first got me thinking about a better way to train salespeople, and that led me to that groundbreaking statement that *every sale is the same.*

At precisely 7 p.m., the meeting started.

It was a meeting that would change the lives of millions of people all over the world, rich and poor alike, and create more top sales producers than every other sales training system combined.

2

INVENTING THE STRAIGHT LINE

"I'M READY TO GO ALL NIGHT," I SAID TO THE STRATTONITES threateningly, and slowly I locked eyes with each and every one of them and let each feel the full weight of my stare. They were sitting behind old wooden desks, arranged classroom-style, and on each desktop sat a cheap black telephone, a gray-colored computer monitor, and a stack of maybe a hundred three-by-five index cards that I'd purchased from Dun & Bradstreet for 22 cents a piece. Each of these cards had the name and phone number of a wealthy investor on it, along with the company they owned and its annual revenue for the prior year.

To Danny and me, these D&Bs, as they were called, were as valuable as gold—with every two hundred cards yielding ten qualified leads, from which we would open between two or three new accounts. And while those numbers might not sound overly impressive, any broker who did that for three straight months would be on pace to make over $2 million per year; and if he did it for a year, he'd be on pace to make more than triple that.

Unfortunately, the Strattonites' results hadn't been quite as impressive. In fact, they'd been downright awful. For every two hundred D&Bs they dialed through, they were averaging only *five* leads, and *from* those five they were closing an average of . . . no one.

Ever.

"So you might as well get comfortable," I continued, "because we're not going anywhere until we figure this out. So let's start by getting brutally honest. I want you guys to tell me why you're finding it so hard to close rich people, because I really don't get it." I shrugged. "I'm doing it! *Danny* is doing it! And I *know* that you guys can do it too." I flashed them a hint of a sympathetic smile. "It's like you have some sort of mental block against this, and it's time to break it down. So, let's start by you guys telling me why this is so *hard* for you? I *really* want to know."

A few moments passed, as I just stood there at the front of the room, looking holes through the Strattonites, who seemed to be literally *shrinking* in their seats under the weight of my stare. They were a motley crew, all right. There was no denying that. It was a miracle that some of these clowns had even passed their broker's exam.

Finally, one of them broke the silence.

"There are too many objections," he whined. "I'm getting hit with them left and right. I can't even get a pitch off!"

"Me too," added another. "There are *thousands* of objections. I can't get a pitch off either. It's a lot harder than with penny stocks."

"Exactly," added a third one. "I'm getting smashed with objections." He let out a deep sigh. "I vote for penny stocks too!"

"Same here," added another. "It's the objections; they don't let up." The rest of the Strattonites began nodding their heads in agreement, as they muttered their collective feelings of disapproval under their breath.

But I wasn't the least bit fazed. With the exception of that one reference about "voting"—*as if this were a fucking democracy!*—I'd heard it all before.

In fact, since the day we'd made the switch, the brokers had been complaining about the increased number of objections and how difficult they were to overcome. And while there was some degree of truth to it, it wasn't *nearly* as difficult as they were making it out to be, not even *close*. *There're thousands of objections?* Give me a break!

For a moment, I considered taking immediate action against the rabble-rousing Strattonite who'd mentioned the V-word, but I decided against it.

It was time to call these guys out on their bullshit, once and for all. "Fair enough," I said, with a hint of sarcasm. "Since you guys are *so* sure about these *thousands* of objections, I want to list every single one of them right now." And, with that, I turned to the whiteboard and grabbed a black Magic Marker off the ledge of the stand and raised it to the center of the board. "Go ahead!" I continued. "Start calling them all out, and then I'll rattle off all the answers for you, one by one, so you can see how easy this is. Come on, let's go!"

The Strattonites began to shift uncomfortably in their seats. They looked utterly dumbfounded, like a family of deer caught in the headlights, but not nearly as cute.

"Come on," I pressed. "Speak now or forever hold your peace."

" 'I want to think about it!' " one finally yelled.

"Good," I replied, and I wrote the objection on the whiteboard. "He wants to think about it. That's a great start. *Keep going.*"

"He wants you to call back!" shouted another.

"Okay," I replied, writing that one down too. "Wants a call back. What else?"

" 'Send me some information!' "

"Okay, that's a good one," I remarked, jotting it down as well. "Keep going. I'll make it easy and we'll shoot for a thousand. There's only 997 to go." I flashed them a sarcastic grin. "It's totally doable."

" 'It's a bad time of year!' " someone yelled.

"Good," I shot back. "Keep going."

" 'I need to speak to my wife!' " yelled another.

"Or his business partner!" shouted yet another.

"Excellent," I said calmly, writing both objections down. "We're making serious progress here. There are only 994 to go. Keep going."

"'I'm not liquid right now!'" yelled a broker.

"Ah, now, *that's* good a one!" I said quickly, scribbling it down on the board. "Although, you have to admit that you're not getting that one quite as much since we started calling rich people. Anyway, let's keep going. There are only 993 to go."

"'I only deal with my local broker!'" one of them yelled.

"'I never heard of your firm before!'" shouted another.

"'I've been burnt before!'"

"'I don't like the market right now!'"

"'I'm too busy!'"

"'I don't trust you!'"

"'I don't make quick decisions!'"

And on and on they went—calling out objection after objection, as I wrote each one down, in progressively worse handwriting. By the time they were done, I'd covered the entire surface of the board with every objection they could possibly think of . . . which, at the end of the day, turned out to be only fourteen.

That's right. There were only *fourteen* objections, and half of them were variations of two: First, that it was a bad time of year, as in it's tax time, summertime, back-to-school time, Christmastime, Miller time, Groundhog Day. And second, that they needed to speak to someone else, as in their spouse, their lawyer, their business partner, their accountant, their local broker, their local soothsayer, their local Tooth Fairy.

What a bunch of crap! I thought.

For the last four weeks, the Strattonites had been going on and on about how impossible it was to deal with these *"thousands of objections,"* to the point where, in my darkest hour, they had almost convinced me that they were right—that there were simply too many objections for the average salesperson to handle and that the success that Danny and I were having was another example of the difference between natural born closers and everyone else. *Yet it had all been a bunch of crap!*

All at once, I felt my face growing hot.

In retrospect, even before I had invented the Straight Line System, I always knew that there wasn't any real difference between one objection and another. But, somehow, seeing them all scribbled out on the whiteboard this way highlighted just how interchangeable they all really were. In fact, it was in that very moment that it *truly* hit me that, at the end of the day, they were all basically the same—that the common objections were nothing more than *smoke screens* for what was *really* holding a prospect back, which was a lack of certainty.

In fact, now that I thought about it, no matter what objection the prospect hit me with, I would never just *answer* it and ask for the order again. That would be pointless, since the objection was merely a *smoke screen* for uncertainty. By itself, in fact, all an answer would do (even a perfect one) is force a prospect to shift to a new objection, because the root problem still hadn't been addressed.

In consequence, after I answered an objection, I would then loop back to the beginning of the sale and make a follow-up presentation that picked up where my initial presentation had left off—with a goal of increasing the prospect's state of certainty for all three Tens. And, once again, as with the rest of my strategies, I would execute each one of my loops in precisely the same exact way, every single time.

It was at that very moment when it suddenly hit me—the idea that every sale was the same. In fact, all at once, that very concept came bubbling up into my brain, followed a millisecond later by an elegantly simple image that I could use to explain it.

The image, as it turned out, was a perfectly straight line.

But that was just the beginning.

Something had *clicked* inside my brain, and a window of clarity had swung open, giving me unfettered access to a seemingly infinite reservoir of what can best be described as pure sales wisdom. I'm talking about radically advanced stuff here—ideas and concepts and tactics and strategies were flashing through my mind at an incredible rate. In my mind's eye, I could see my own sales strategy being pulled apart, into its elemental pieces, and then put back together, in exactly the right order, along a perfectly straight line. My heart literally skipped a beat. It happened so fast that it seemed almost *instantaneous*, but it hit me with the force of an atomic bomb.

Until that very moment, I simply hadn't known why I had been able to far outsell every other salesperson, at every single company I had ever worked for. But now I knew.

My own sales strategy, which had been mostly *unconscious* until then, had suddenly become conscious. I could see each distinct chunk of my strategy, as if it had the defined edges of a jigsaw piece, and each individual piece seemed to be screaming out its purpose at me. But there was more—*much, much more.*

When I shifted my focus to any particular piece, I suddenly had access to every root experience and every memory that justified the piece's purpose and location; and by focusing a bit deeper, a torrent of words came gushing into my consciousness, providing the perfect explanation for the piece and how it related to the others.

For example, if I looked at the point on the line marked "sales presentation," then I immediately knew that there were three things that had to be addressed before the prospect would say yes; and then, if I focused a bit harder, the word "certainty" popped into my mind, followed, a millisecond later, by each of the Three Tens, which seemed to be floating above the line and tethered to scenes going back all the way to my childhood, of random sales situations I had been in on either side, as salesperson or prospect, and a vivid memory of why I had said no or yes to the salespeople, or the prospects had said no or yes to me.

All of those things, each compressed into a millisecond, had flashed through my brain while I stood before the whiteboard, staring at the objections. From end to end, the entire experience was maybe one or two seconds, but when I turned to face the Strattonites I was an entirely different person.

As I scanned their faces, the strengths and weaknesses of each came popping into my brain in a singular rush of thoughts, as did a perfect way to train each of them to perfection. In short, I would teach them to sell exactly the way I did—by taking immediate control of the sale, and then moving the prospect from the open to the close along the shortest distance between any two points: a straight line.

With renewed confidence, I said, "Don't you guys get it? Every sale is the same!"

All twelve Strattonites shot me confused looks.

I ignored them, with relish, and I unleashed my discovery.

"*Watch,*" I said forcefully. "It's a straight line!" And I turned back to the whiteboard, and for the very first time, I drew that long, thin horizontal line across the middle of it and placed a big, thick X on either end.

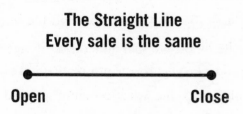

The Straight Line
Every sale is the same

Open   **Close**

"Now, this is your open"—I pointed to the X on the left end of the line—"where the sale begins, and this is your close"—I pointed to the X on the right end of the line—"where the prospect says, 'Yeah, let's do it,' and he opens up the account with you.

"The key here is that, from literally the *first* word out of your mouth, everything you say and everything you do is designed to keep your prospect *on* the straight line, and slowly nudge him forward, from the open to the close. You guys follow me so far?"

The Strattonites nodded in unison. The room was so quiet you could have heard a pin drop. The air felt *electric*.

"Good," I replied quickly. "Now, as a salesperson, every once in a while, we get one of those *perfect*, lay-down sales, where the prospect seems to be almost *pre-sold* before we even open up our mouths." As I continued to speak, I began drawing tiny arrows on the center of the line, starting just after the left X, and then moving down the line, to just before the X on the right. "It's one of those sales where everything you say, and everything you do, and every case you make about why the prospect should buy from you, he keeps on saying, *yes, yes, yes,* without giving you even a single objection, right up to the moment where you ask him for the order, and he agrees to close. That's what I mean by a perfect straight-line sale.

Open   **Close**

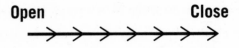

"Who's ever had one of those perfect, lay-down sales, where the client seemed to be almost pre-sold from the start? You all have, right?" I raised my right hand, prompting them to do the same.

All twelve hands quickly shot up.

"Of course you have," I said confidently. "The *problem* is that those sales are far and few between. Typically, what happens is that your prospect keeps trying to take you *off* the straight line and take control of the conversation." I drew a series of thin arrows, pointing upward and downward (↑↓), *away* from the straight line, to illustrate that point.

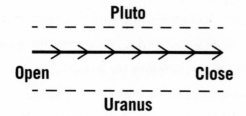

"So, basically, you want to keep the prospect *on* the straight line, moving forward towards the close, and he keeps trying to take you *off* the straight line, and spiral off to Pluto"—I wrote the word "Pluto" near the top of the whiteboard—"or down here, to *Your-anus*"—I wrote the word "Your-anus" near the bottom of the whiteboard—"which is not a very good place to be, at least for most of you." I threw my hands in the air and shrugged, as if to say, "To each his own!"

"So what we have are these healthy boundaries, above and below the line—one *here* and one *here*," I continued, drawing two dotted lines that were parallel to the straight line, one of them six inches above it, and the other six inches below it.

"When you're *inside* the boundaries, you're in control of the sale, and moving forward towards the close. When you're *outside* the boundaries, the client is in control and you're spiraling off to Pluto, or down *here*, to Your-anus, where you're talking about the price of tea in China or politics in America or some other irrelevant topic that's not germane to the sale.

"And, by the way, I hear you guys doing this shit *all* the time when I walk around the room, and it drives me fucking *crazy*!" I shook my head gravely. "Seriously—ninety percent of the time you guys are off in freaking Pluto, talking about some nonsense that has nothing to do with the stock market." I closed my eyes tightly and gave my head a few quick shakes back and forth, as if to say, "Some things just completely defy logic!" Then I said, "Anyway, I know what you guys are thinking—that the more time you spend *bullshitting* with these people, the more rapport you end up building.

"Well, I've got a news flash for you," I continued sarcastically. "You're *wrong*. People see through that shit in two seconds flat, especially *rich people*, who are constantly on guard for that. To them, it's actually *repulsive*, not attractive, which is the opposite of what building rapport is all about." I shrugged. "Anyway, it doesn't really matter, because you guys are done with that shit, *now*. It's *over*.

"I'm going to teach you guys how to take control of the sale tonight, the way *I* do it, and how I taught Danny to do it; and that means you're going to stay inside these boundaries, here and here. This is where you're *in control. Boom, boom!*" I banged my right knuckle on two spots inside the boundaries, one above the line and one below, and I marked each spot with the initials IC.

"And *here* and *here*: this is where you're *out* of control." And I banged my right knuckle on two spots *outside* of the boundaries, one above the top dotted line and one below the bottom dotted line, and then I marked each space with the initials OC.

"In control, out of control," I repeated, tapping the respective initials.

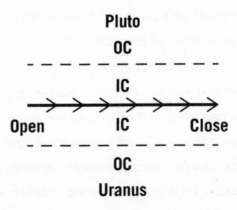

"Now, when you're *on* the straight line—meaning, directly on it— that's where *you're* doing all the talking. And all these little arrows here: the reason they're all pointing *down* the line, to the close"—I began tapping the tip of my marker on each arrow, as I continued speaking, starting with the very first arrow, just after the open, and moving quickly to the right, all the way down to the close—"is because with every single word you say there's one specific goal in mind, and that's to move the prospect *down* the straight line towards the close; that's it. There are no free words, no time for stupid statements, and no time to go off to Pluto and talk about the price of tea in China.

"*That* shit is for *novices*." My obvious contempt for novices dripped off the very word. "When *you're* speaking, it's *directed*. It's powerful. Your words have *meaning* behind them; and the meaning is to create *massive* certainty in the mind of your prospect as you move him down the straight line, from the open to the close." I pointed to the arrows again. "That's why every one of these arrows is *compact*, and *tight*, and *right on the line*—and they're all pointed straight towards the close.

"So, again, that's what's happening when you're directly *on* the straight line. You're the one doing all the talking, and your client is listening. And when you're *off* the straight line, but still inside the boundaries, right here and here"—I point to the spaces—"it's the prospect who's doing the talking, and you're doing the listening.

"And, by the way, this is where some really great stuff happens— when you're actually *off* the straight line, right in those spaces. In fact, there's not one, but two absolutely crucial things happening here.

"First, you're developing immediate, massive rapport, on both a conscious *and* unconscious level; and second, you're gathering massive intelligence, which up until tonight, I used to refer to as *qualifying*. But, starting right now, I want you to wipe that word out of your mind forever, because it doesn't even come *close* to describing what we need to accomplish here.

"You see, with the Straight Line, you need to *gather intelligence*—and I mean *massive intelligence*—which goes far beyond trying to figure out whether or not a prospect is financially qualified.

"When you gather *intelligence* from a prospect, you're doing all of the following things:

"**First**, you're identifying their needs—and not just their core need but also any secondary needs or 'problems' they might have.

"**Second**, you're identifying any core beliefs they might have that could impact the sale, such as not feeling comfortable working over the phone or with making quick decisions, and also not trusting salespeople in general.

"**Third**, you want to find out about any past experiences they've had with similar products, both good and bad, and how they feel about the salespeople they bought them from.

"**Fourth**, you want to identify their values—meaning, what things are most important to them? Are they looking for growth or income, or do they want to set themselves up for retirement, or to give their profits to a certain charity, or a religious institution? It can even be that the prospect is an action junkie and they're in it for the thrills.

"**Fifth**, you want to identify their financial standards, insofar as what level of wealth and spending ability they need to have to feel good about themselves.

"**Sixth**, where their pain lies—meaning, what's keeping them up at night? What's that one single financial worry that sits at the very base of their skull and weighs them down, like an anchor?

"You see, at the end of the day, it's knowing your prospect's pain and, if necessary, amplifying that pain; if they're currently in denial, that's going to help you close the tougher sales.

"And **seventh**, you need to identify where they stand financially, in terms of how much money they have in the market right now, how liquid they are, how much money they typically invest into an idea they like, and how much they are liquid for overall.

"So, getting back to the Straight Line:

"When you're off the line, you're looking to (a) continue building on the rapport that you already have, and (b) use that rapport to help you gather the more *invasive* intelligence, like how liquid the prospect currently is.

"And at the same time, you're always making sure that the encounter stays within the boundaries, as you continue the process of moving the sale down the Straight Line, towards the close.

"Essentially, those are the three basic tenets of the front half of the Straight Line:

1 You must take immediate of control the sale.

2 You must engage in massive intelligence gathering, while you simultaneously build massive rapport with your prospect.

3 You must smoothly transition into a Straight Line presentation, so you can begin the process of building absolute certainty for each of the Three Tens.

"So, again, during the front half of the sale, you first take immediate control of the sale; then you use that control to gather massive intelligence, which entails asking highly specific questions, which I'll map out for you in advance, to make sure that you've gathered all the intelligence you need—and I'm going to circle back to this later, because, starting tomorrow, you're going to be asking a lot more questions than you used to.

"And next, as you're *gathering* all this intelligence, you're going to do it in a way that allows you to build massive rapport with your prospect at the same time, which is absolutely crucial, by the way, because the questions you'll be asking him are going to get more and more invasive as you move along.

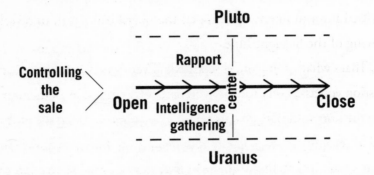

"And then, after you ask for the order for the first time, which happens right around here, while you're still close to the beginning"—I pointed to a spot on the line about a third of the way towards the close, and punctuated it by drawing a big, thick black dot—"that's where the back-half of the sale begins, when you get hit with your first objection. So, obviously, this whole front-half-back-half-business is merely a figure of speech." I shrugged.

"I mean, I can teach a frickin' *monkey* to read from a script and ask for the order; so don't think that you've accomplished anything amazing because you made it through the front half of the sale; it's the back half of the sale where the *real* selling begins! This is when you finally get the chance to roll up your sleeves and get down to cases—meaning, to get to the bottom of what's really holding your prospect back, which is certainly not the objection they gave you; that's merely a smoke screen for uncertainty!

"And the objection could be any one of these." I grabbed the top right edge of the whiteboard and flipped the board over, revealing the fourteen common objections.

"They want to think about it or call you back or talk to their wife or do some research or it's a bad time of year; it doesn't matter which one they give you. In the end, they're all basically the same; they're smoke screens for uncertainty! In other words, your prospect still isn't certain enough to say yes, which means you've still got some selling left to do." I paused for a moment and flipped the board back over, to reveal my drawing of the Straight Line.

"That's what's going on," I repeated. "Every word, every phrase, every question you ask, every tonality you use; every single one of them should have the same ultimate goal in mind, which is to increase the prospect's level of certainty *as much as humanly possible*, so that by the time you get to the close, he's feeling so incredibly certain that he almost *has* to say yes. That's your goal.

"In fact, think of this as *goal-oriented communication*," I continued, spitting out the phrase at literally the same instant it popped into my mind. "Every word that comes out of your mouth is feeding into one single goal, which is to increase your prospect's level of certainty to the highest possible level, as you're moving him down the straight line towards the close. Here—let me draw it out for you on the board.

"Imagine a *continuum of certainty* between one and ten," I said confidently. As I began turning back to the whiteboard, I saw one of the Strattonite's hands shoot up. It was Colton Green.

Colton Green was an eighteen-year-old Irishman, with a beefy skull, a budding drinker's nose, and an IQ just above the level of an idiot. A nincompoop among nincompoops! But a lovable nincompoop, nonetheless.

With a dead smile: "Green?"

"What's a continuum?" he asked.

The rest of the Strattonites chuckled at Colton's idiocy, which was rather ironic, I thought, considering that most of them were idiots too.

But, as it turned out, the usual deterrents to success, such as idiocy and stupidity, were about to become completely irrelevant inside the four walls of Stratton's boardroom.

You see, over those next few hours, I literally *invented* the Straight Line System as I was teaching it to the Strattonites. The system effortlessly poured out of me, with each breakthrough paving the way for yet another breakthrough. I felt as if I were almost channeling the information from some place else, a place of infinite knowledge and infinite wisdom, a place where the answers to all of my questions, no matter how complex, were ready and waiting, and there for the taking. So I took all that I could, with relish.

By midnight, I had laid out the framework for the entire system, and had created the first Straight Line Syntax. Consisting of eight distinct steps, the syntax served as a simple road map for taking a prospect down the straight line. It showed the Strattonites what to do first, what to do second, what to do third . . . all the way down to the eighth and final step, where the prospect either said yes, and opened an account with you, or he stuck to whatever objection he'd been using as his smoke screen, and you ended the call, respectfully, and moved on to the next prospect.

About a month later, I added on two additional steps, as deeper layers of the system continued to pour out of me; then, many years later, I increased the number to fourteen, when I created the 2.0 version of the Straight Line System and began teaching it around the world. Amazingly, though, the *core* of the syntax remains almost identical to what came out of me that first Tuesday evening, which makes perfect sense when you consider what happened the next morning, when the Strattonites hit the phones armed with the Straight Line System for the very first time. In fact, if I hadn't seen it with my own eyes, I wouldn't have believed it.

From literally the *moment* they started dialing, the entire office went on an account-opening spree of such biblical proportions that, within 90 days, every last one of them had become a million-dollar producer.

But that was only the beginning.

As word of our success began to spread, brokers began showing up at my door unannounced.

By the end of 1989, there were more than 200 Strattonites working in one massive boardroom at Stratton's new corporate headquarters in Lake Success, Long Island.

Twice a day, every day, I would stand before a rapidly expanding army of obscenely young Strattonites and pound them with a combination of Straight Line skills training and daily motivation. In essence, by radically enhancing their mind-sets and skill-sets, I was able to persuade each new Strattonite to leave the insults of the past behind and check their *emotional baggage* at the door; to accept the fact that the moment they stepped into the boardroom everything in the past fell off.

Day after day, I told them that their past did not equal their future, unless they choose to live there. I told them that if they fully embraced the Straight Line System and simply picked up the phone and said the words I taught them, they could become as powerful as the most powerful CEO in America.

And I told them to *act as if.*

I said, "Act as if you're a wealthy man, rich already, and you will become rich. Act as if you have unmatched confidence, and you will become confident. Act as if you have all the answers and the answers will come to you!"

I told them to act as if their success was a foregone conclusion—that it was time to accept the fact that they had *true* greatness inside them, greatness that had always been there, dying to come out, but it had been buried under countless layers of insults and bullshit that society had dumped on them, in an effort to keep them down and make them settle for a life of mediocrity and averagism.

And while all those thoughts were still fresh in their mind, I would set up my transition, focusing on the dire importance of skills training by getting brutally honest with them. I would say, "Maybe some of the stuff that people said about you *was* actually true. Maybe your parents and your teachers and your ex-boss, and ex-girlfriend—maybe they were all *right* about you. Maybe you're not that special?

"Maybe you were born just an *average* guy: not all that smart, not very well-spoken, not overly motivated; and you slept through grade school, you cheated your way through high school, you didn't go to college. So maybe you've had the *desire* to achieve greatness, but you truly weren't capable of it. You lacked the skills you needed to go out into the world and kick some ass!

"Now, be honest here, how many of you guys feel like that sometimes? Not always, but *sometimes*, like when you're lying in bed at night, alone with your thoughts, and the fears and the negativity come out and start whispering in your ear, eating away at your self-confidence and self-worth? Raise your hand if you feel like that sometimes."

Like clockwork, every hand in the room would go flying up.

"Exactly," I'd continue. "Most people feel that way; and they actually have *every* right to . . . because they're *not* special! They *don't* have any special skill or talent or ability that sets them apart from everyone else; they have no *edge*, no advantage that they can use to separate themselves from the pack, nothing they can use to get rich.

"And, by the way, I hate to say it, but that includes pretty much every one of you in this room." Then I'd quickly add the punch line. "Or at least it used to.

"See, I don't know if you guys actually get this, so let me make it crystal clear for you: you are *not* the same person who walked into this boardroom on your first day. In fact, you're not even *close* to being the same person! The Straight Line System has *changed you*! It's made you an infinitely more effective human being than you've ever been in your entire life—because you now own a skill that sets you apart from pretty much everyone else on the planet: you have the ability to close the deal, to influence and persuade at the highest possible level, to the point where you can close anyone who's closable.

"And since you didn't *own* this skill *before*, anything negative that happened to you in the past has absolutely no bearing on the future. Do you understand that? Do you see the *power* in that? Do you guys realize that every last one of you has turned yourself into a force of nature? Someone who can create any vision for the future they want and then go out and achieve it. The simple fact is that the ability to close the deal is the single most important distinction, bar none, when it comes to achieving wealth and success, and you guys literally own that skill at the highest level. And if you think I'm making this shit up or even *exaggerating*, then go ask any rich person and they'll tell you, *straight away*, that without the ability to close the deal, it is *really* hard to make money; and once you *do* have that ability, then everything becomes easy.

"In fact, that's why I can point to any person in this room who's been here for more than a few months, and he'll tell you some ridiculous success story that no one *outside* of this room would even believe, because the success is so extreme that they can't even wrap their arms around it . . . ," and on and on I would go, day in and day out, once in the morning, before the market opened, and then again in the afternoon, after it closed. I kept pounding the Strattonites with a twice-daily combination of skills training and motivation; and with each passing day the success stories grew crazier and crazier.

By the end of year one, top producers were earning over $250,000 a month, and their success seemed to be almost *contagious*. Even par had climbed to $100,000 a month, and the attrition rate was basically zero. In other words, if you made it into the boardroom, then you were almost *guaranteed* to succeed. All you had to do was take a quick look around you, in any direction, and there was massive success everywhere.

For a new trainee, this was more than sufficient to quash any doubts about the power and effectiveness of the Straight Line System. In fact, after a few months of teaching it, I had devised a paint-by-number training curriculum that was so easy to follow that it was virtually foolproof.

Five Core Elements of the Straight Line System

At the heart of the system are five core elements. To this very day, they're exactly the same as the day I created them, and they serve as the backbone of the entire system.

As you may have guessed, I've already touched on the first three elements, namely, the all-important Three Tens:

1 The prospect must *love* your product.

2 The prospect must trust and connect with *you*.

3 The prospect must trust and connect with your company.

In essence, as you move your prospect down the straight line, everything you say should be specifically designed to *increase* your prospect's level of certainty for at least one of the three elements—with your *ultimate* goal being to move all *three* of them to as close to a 10 as possible, at which point you're going to ask for the order and hopefully close the deal.

However, that being said, what you need to remember here is that this is not the type of process that happens all at once. In fact, in the *vast* majority of cases, you're going to have to ask for the order at least two or three times before you have any chance of your prospect saying yes.

Now, when you finish the main body of your sales presentation, you've reached a point on the Straight Line where you are going to ask for the order for the first time and wait for a response—and then the back half of the sale begins, which gets triggered when the prospect hits you with the first objection. Alternatively, this is the point in the sale where you'll find out if you have a lay-down on your hands, in which case the prospect will simply say yes, and you can close the deal without having to address any objections.

But, as I said before, these lay-down sales are few and far between. Most of the time, prospects are going to hit you with at least one or two objections, although *usually* it's more like three of four.

IN ORDER TO MOVE FORWARD THE PROSPECT NEEDS A HIGH LEVEL OF CERTAINTY

But, either way, since these objections are actually smoke screens for uncertainty, the salesperson has to be prepared to not only answer them in a way that satisfies the prospect but also make a follow-up presentation that picks up right where the initial presentation left off—with a goal of increasing the prospect's level of certainty for the Three Tens even further, and with an ultimate goal of getting the prospect as close as possible to a "10, 10, 10," both logically and emotionally, which gives the salesperson the best possible chance of closing the deal. The Straight Line technique that we use to accomplish this is called *looping*.

Looping is a simple yet highly effective objection-handling strategy that allows a salesperson to take each individual objection and use it as an opportunity to further increase a prospect's level of certainty, without breaking rapport, and then seamlessly transition into a close.

In many ways, the art of looping is the so-called "secret sauce" to the Straight Line System (or at least to the *back half* of it)—as it allows a salesperson to increase a prospect's level of certainty in small increments, as opposed to all at once.

In other words, each objection creates the opportunity to loop; and each loop results in a further increase to a prospect's level of certainty; and as each loop is completed, the prospects find themselves that much farther down the line, and that much closer to the close.

While looping is a very simple process, there is one particular scenario that keeps coming up again and again, and unless a salesperson is prepared for it, it tends to drive them up the wall.

For the most part, this scenario rears its ugly head after you've run two or three loops, and you've raised your prospect's level of certainty to a point where they're so *absolutely* certain that you can actually hear it both in their tone of voice and the actual words they say.

In short, the prospect has made it crystal clear to you through their words, their tonality, and, if you're in person, their body language that they are absolutely certain about all of the Three Tens; yet, for some inexplicable reason, they are still not buying.

There's actually a very logical reason for this, and it has to do with an invisible force that holds sway over every sales encounter—dictating how far down the line a salesperson has to take any particular prospect before they finally say yes; or, put another way, at what collective level of certainty does any particular prospect need to be at before he or she says yes?

You see, at the end of the day, not all prospects are created equal. There are some who are very tough to sell to; others who are very easy to sell to; and still others who are right in the middle, being neither tough nor easy. When you dig beneath the surface, it turns out that what separates all these potential buyers from one another is the sum of the individual beliefs they have about buying, about making decisions in general, and about trusting other people, especially those who are trying to sell them things.

Together, the sum of all these beliefs, and all the experiences that have contributed to the formation of these beliefs, creates a defined "threshold of certainty" that a prospect must cross over before he or she feels comfortable enough to buy.

We call this level of certainty a person's *action threshold*, and it comprises the fourth core element of the Straight Line System. By way of definition, we refer to people who are very easy to sell to as having a *low action threshold*; and we refer to people who are very difficult to sell to as having a *high action threshold*.

Now, that's all fine and dandy, but what makes this concept so absolutely crucial to a salesperson's success is a remarkable discovery I made that proved to be the linchpin strategy that allowed people with very little natural sales ability to close at the same level as a natural born salesperson, namely: that a prospect's action threshold is *malleable*; it is not set in stone.

Practically speaking, the implications of this are staggering. After all, if you can lower a person's action threshold, then you can turn some of the toughest buyers into easy buyers—which is something that we do with *great* effect in the latter stages of the sale, and that sets up the possibility of being able to close anyone who is closeable.

However, when you're out in the field, you're going to find some extraordinarily tough customers. I'm talking about prospects who still won't buy from you, *even* after you've raised their level of certainty as much as humanly possible, and then lowered their action threshold and asked for the order again.

So, for these ultra-tough nuts to crack, we now turn to the fifth core element of the Straight Line System: the *pain threshold.*

You see, at the end of the day, pain is the most powerful motivator of all—causing human beings to quickly move away from whatever they believe is the source of their pain, and to move towards whatever they believe will resolve their pain. In essence, pain creates urgency, which makes it the perfect vehicle for closing these tougher sales.

To that end it's absolutely crucial that you take the time to uncover precisely what your prospect's pain is and where it comes from. Once I have that information, I can then position my product as a *remedy* for their pain, and then verbally paint a picture for them of the future—showing how much better they are going to feel as a result of using my product, which has taken away all their pain and has them feeling pleasure again.

In addition, by saving this powerful human motivator for last, it gives us the ability to make that one final push—taking a prospect who needs our product and wants our product and can truly benefit from our product—and creating just enough pain to push them across their action threshold and get them to buy.

So, there you have it:

THE FIVE CORE ELEMENTS OF THE STRAIGHT LINE SYSTEM

1 The prospect must *love* your product.

2 The prospect must trust and connect with *you*.

3 The prospect must trust and connect with your company.

4 Lower the action threshold.

5 Raise the pain threshold.

Each of these core elements serves its own unique purpose, while paving the way for everything that comes after it.

My favorite metaphor to explain this process is how a professional safecracker goes about plying his trade, like in the movie *The Italian Job*. If you haven't seen it, here's the skinny:

Donald Sutherland plays one of those old-fashioned safecrackers, who puts his ear to the tumbler and listens for each click. Upon hearing the first one, he spins the tumbler in the opposite direction and waits for the next one, and then the next one, and then the next one after that. Finally, when he's gotten a click for each number in the combination, he'll pull down the handle to try and open the safe and—*voilà!*—if he's identified each number correctly, the safe will open.

In a manner of speaking, that's precisely what you're doing when you're moving a prospect down the Straight Line. Essentially, you're cracking the code to his or her buying combination, and you're doing it the same way every single time.

And here's what we know about the "safe" of the human brain, when it comes to making a buying decision: there are only five numbers in the combination; that's it!

The first number is a prospect's level of certainty about your *product*; the second number is their level of certainty about *you*; the third number is their level of certainty about your *company*; the fourth number addresses their action threshold; and the fifth number addresses their pain threshold.

That's all there is: five basic numbers to crack.

Now, in terms of how we spin the tumbler, well . . . that's what the next 200 pages of this book are about. In that regard, I guess it's fair to say that this book is basically a universal safecracker's manual for the human mind.

Will it crack every single buying combination?

No, not every one; and that's a good thing.

After all, not everyone is closable, at least not on *every* occasion, and sometimes it turns out, due to ethical reasons, a prospect shouldn't be closed. That said, however, what the Straight Line System *can* do, once you become reasonably proficient at it, is get you to a point where you can close anyone who's closable.

In other words, if someone doesn't buy from you, then you'll know that it wasn't because you did something wrong. You won't walk away from a sale saying to yourself, "Too bad JB wasn't here; he would've closed him!"

However, as powerful as the Straight Line System is, it completely breaks down in the absence of one crucial element, which is: *You need to take immediate control of the sale.*

Without control, it's like you're an amateur boxer stepping into the ring with Mike Tyson. Within seconds, you'd be completely on the defensive, covering up from Tyson's massive blows, until one finally slips through, and you get knocked out.

Yet, from Tyson's perspective, because he took immediate control of the encounter, from literally the moment the bell rang, he won the fight by knockout before it had even started—same as he did in the last fight, and the fight before that, and the fight before that.

Put another way, by taking immediate control of each fight he was able to make *every fight the same*. Slowly but surely, he maneuvered his opponent into a corner, cutting off every possible escape; then he softened him up with body blows and waited for him to drop his hands; and then—*bam!*—he'd land the exact knockout punch that he'd been planning all along.

In the first Straight Line syntax, and in each syntax that followed, taking immediate control of the sale was the very first step in the system, and it always will be.

Just how you go about doing that turned out to be elegantly simple, albeit with one complication:

You have only four seconds to do it.

Otherwise, you're *toast*.

3

THE FIRST FOUR SECONDS

FOR BETTER OR WORSE, WE HAVE TO ACCEPT THE FACT THAT, AS human beings, we're basically fear-based creatures. We're constantly sizing up our surroundings and making snap decisions based on how we perceive them. Is it safe? Is there danger nearby? Do we need to be extra careful about something?

This type of snap decision-making goes all the way back to our caveman days, and it's wired into our reptilian brains. When we saw something back then, we had to size it up instantly and decide whether to stay or run. It was only *after* we were sure that we were safe that we'd start debating whether or not it made sense to stick around for a potential benefit.

That quick decision-making instinct is still with us today. The stakes are much lower, of course, because we don't typically face life-or-death situations every day. But, still, the process happens just as quickly. In fact, it happens in less than four seconds over the phone, and in only a *quarter* of a second when you're in person. That's how fast the brain reacts.

Think about that: it takes only a quarter of a second for a prospect to make an initial decision about you when you meet them in person. We know this because scientists have conducted experiments where they hook people up to a certain type of MRI machine that reveals how the brain works as it's processing information. Here's what happens when scientists flash a test subject a picture of someone: first, the subject's visual cortex lights up almost instantly, and then, a quarter of a second later, their prefrontal lobe lights up, which is where the judgment center of the brain is located, and a decision gets made. It happens *that* quickly.

During a phone call with a prospect, you have a bit longer—you have four seconds to make an impression.

To be clear, though, even when you're in person, it still takes four seconds before a *final* judgment gets made. The difference is that the process starts sooner when you're in person—literally from the first moment the prospect lays eyes on you. But, either way, whether in person or over the phone, there are three things that you *need to* establish in those first four seconds of an encounter, if you want to be perceived in just the right way:

1 **Sharp as a tack**

2 **Enthusiastic as hell**

3 **An expert in your field**

Those three things absolutely *must* come across in the first four seconds of a conversation; otherwise, you set yourself up for a major uphill battle.

Now, in truth, if you screw up the first four seconds, you have another ten seconds, at most, to play catch-up ball, but after that, you're completely done. It's basically a lost cause. You can't influence anybody.

At this point you might be asking yourself, "What happened to not judging a book by its cover? What about *that*, Jordan?"

Well, my parents were actually big believers in that adage, and so were my schoolteachers.

But you know what?

They did it, and so do *I*; and so do *you*, for that matter. Each and every one of us judges books by their covers. It's basically hardwired into our brains; and it's not just an American thing; it's also an Australian thing, a Chinese thing, a Brazilian thing; an Italian thing—it's a *human* thing. It exists everywhere in the world, and crosses all cultural boundaries.

The bottom line is that you have four seconds until someone rips you apart, compartmentalizes you, judges each piece, and then puts you back together again based on how you were perceived. And if those three aforementioned things—being sharp as a tack, enthusiastic as hell, and an expert in your field—haven't been established firmly in your prospect's mind, then you have basically no chance of closing them.

Now, why is that?

Well, think about it for a second: do you really want to do business with a *novice*? When you go buy a car or a stock or a computer, who do you want guiding you through the process, a novice or an expert? An *expert*, of course!

In fact, we've been conditioned since we were *yea* big to seek out experts to help us solve our problems and eliminate our pain. When we were sick, our parents took us to a very special person called a doctor, who wore a white lab coat and had a stethoscope around their neck; and we were awestruck, at first, at how even our *own parents* deferred to this person—until they told us why. This person, they explained, had been through countless years of schooling, during which they learned everything there was to know about making sick people feel better. These people were even taught how to dress and how to act and how to talk so people would have confidence in them at a single glance, which is why you started to feel better just by being in their presence. This person had earned the right to be called a doctor, because they were a true expert in their field.

But, of course, this was only the beginning of our conditioning. As we grew older, the parade of experts continued.

If we were struggling in school, our parents might hire us a tutor; if we wanted to master a certain sport, they'd hire us a coach. And when we entered adulthood, we picked up right where our parents left off, and to this very day we continue to seek out experts and teach our children to do the same.

Think about it for a moment.

Who do you think Scarlett Johansson wants styling her hair on the day of the Oscars? Is she going to seek out some pimple-faced kid who's fresh out of beauty school, or is she going to track down the world's foremost stylist, who's been making celebrities look fabulous for the last twenty years?

And who do you think Jordan Spieth or Jason Day will turn to if they're in a slump: a local pro at a municipal course or a world-famous swing doctor who's written books on the subject and who's worked with other famous professionals for at least twenty years?

The simple fact is that we *all* want to deal with pros or experts, and we also want to deal with people who are sharp and on the ball, and who are enthusiastic about what they do. Experts have a certain way of talking that literally *commands* respect. They say things like "Listen, Bill, you need to trust me on this. I've been doing this for fifteen years, and I know exactly what you need."

Novices, on the other hand, tend to speak in far less definite terms, and their limited grasp on the deeper nuances of their product and their particular industry becomes more and more apparent as they move a prospect farther down the Straight Line and enter the looping phase, and are forced to "free-form"—meaning, they run out of scripted material and are forced to make things up on the fly in an effort to push their prospect's level of certainty above their action threshold so they'll buy.

My point here is that how you are perceived will carry through to every part of the sale, but it starts in the first four seconds. If you screw that up and make a negative first impression, then you basically have no chance of closing the deal.

Interestingly, the first time I said this was close to thirty years ago, on that very Tuesday evening when I invented the Straight Line System. I told the Strattonites that evening that they had precisely four seconds to make that all-important first impression.

However, as it turns out, I was actually wrong.

In 2013, a professor at Harvard University published a study on this exact topic—the importance of first impressions—and what the study found was that it wasn't four seconds until a prospect made the initial judgment; it was actually *five* seconds. So I have to apologize for being off by one second.

Apologies aside, what the study *also* found was that if you make a negative first impression, it takes *eight* subsequent positive impressions to erase that one negative first impression. Frankly, I don't know about you, but in all my years in sales, and with all the products I've sold, I can't think of one industry where, if I screwed up the first meeting, I got eight subsequent chances to redeem myself. It simply doesn't happen.

That's why it is absolutely mandatory to establish those three crucial elements in the first four seconds of the conversation, every single time. Otherwise, you're toast.

1 **First, you're sharp as a tack.** If they don't think that you're sharp as a tack, you're wasting their time. You must come across as someone who's totally on the ball, a born problem-solver who is definitely worth listening to because you can help them achieve their goals. In essence, you have to sound and act like someone who can help the prospect fulfill their needs and desires. You can accomplish this by demonstrating

mental speed and agility, fast decision-making, and a unique pace of delivery that immediately impresses the prospect and builds trust.

However, to achieve lasting success, you must actually *become* an "expert in your field," so that you do, indeed, know what you're talking about. In other words, you can't just talk the talk; you also have to walk the walk. So while you're busy "acting as if," you're working at lightning speed to learn everything there is to know about your industry and the products you're selling, so you truly *do* become an expert.

2 **Second, you're enthusiastic as hell.** This sends a subliminal message to your prospect, telling them that you must have something great to offer. You must sound upbeat, enthusiastic, and full of energy, and be a positive influence in their lives. One of things that I had to learn the hard way was that just because you can sell someone something doesn't necessarily mean that you should.

Today, I have a strong belief in sales as an honorable profession, and I'll only operate in sales situations where I have an unyielding and passionate belief in the value of the product or service I'm offering to prospects. I need to genuinely believe in that value before I sell a product or service, and then I'll describe it passionately. I also have to have a firm belief in the company that the product and I represent. This is what allows me to act enthusiastically in any sales situation.

3 **Third, you're an expert in your field—an authority figure and a force to be reckoned with.** From the time they're old enough to walk, people are taught to respect and listen to authority figures. In sales situations, I convince the prospect that I am a highly competent, ultraknowledgeable professional by coming off as a world-class expert in my field, right out of the gate. Not only does this allow me to instantly gain the prospect's respect, but it also causes them to defer to me and basically hand over control of the sale.

To demonstrate this authority, I translate features of the service or product into benefits and value for the prospect, while using technical industry lingo that I've taken the time to simplify—allowing the prospect to easily grasp what appear to be very complex statements. I'll also add value by offering a unique perspective during the sales conversation, demonstrating extensive knowledge and understanding of the market, industry, product, prospect, and competitors.

Remember, the biggest misconception among new salespeople is that they feel like they have to wait a certain amount of time until they can brand themselves as an expert. That's a load of crap! You need to be "acting as if" from the very start, while you *educate* yourself as fast possible, to close the knowledge gap.

Show Them You're Worth Listening To

When you immediately establish these three things, they roll up into one simple fact in the prospect's mind, namely *that you're a person worth listening to.* In other words, it makes sense for them to take time out of their busy day, because someone who's as sharp as you and enthusiastic as you, and who's achieved your level of expertise, is going to:

1 **Get to the point quickly**

2 **Not waste the prospect's time**

3 **Have a solution to their problem**

4 **Be an asset to them over the long-term**

In addition, once the prospect has come to this positive conclusion about you, their brain will instantly extrapolate your value to its logical end, which is:

You can help them achieve their goals.

You can help get them what they want in life.

It could be a core need they're looking to fulfill; it could be a simple want or desire; it could be to gain control over a certain aspect of their life; or, at the *highest* level, it could be to alleviate a *pain* they're feeling.

And, again, because the human brain is so naturally adept at this, it takes less than four short seconds for your prospect to rip you apart, analyze each piece of you, and then put you back together based on how you were perceived.

If you're perceived the *right* way—that you're sharp as a tack, enthusiastic as hell, and an expert in your field—then the prospect will defer to you and let you take control of the sale.

If you're perceived the *wrong* way—that you're as dull as dishwater, a disinterested bore, and a stone-cold novice—then the opposite happens and the prospect takes control. It's nothing less than a make-or-break situation.

Now, that being said, one thing that I want to make *crystal clear* to you is that I am not advocating that you become one of those talking-head types, the kind who go on and on while their prospect just sits there and listens.

While that might be what pops into your mind when I say, "take control of the sale," I assure you that this is not what I'm talking about. I mean, think about it for a second: don't you utterly *despise* being on the receiving end of a salesperson who goes on and on without ever letting you speak?

It makes me want to run out the door!

That's why the Straight Line System is as much about becoming an expert *listener* as an expert talker.

However, to truly become an *expert listener*, you *first* need to learn how to take immediate control of the sale. There's simply no other way.

The million-dollar question is *how*?

4

TONALITY AND BODY LANGUAGE

SO LET'S GET DOWN TO BRASS TACKS.

How do you convince your prospects that you're sharp as a tack, enthusiastic as hell, and an expert in your field, in the first four seconds of a conversation?

In fact, let me take it one step further:

Since a substantial portion of communication takes place over the phone nowadays, how do you ensure that you're being perceived the right way when your prospects can't even *see* you?

Is it through the words you say?

Think about that for a moment. What could you say to try to get all that across in those first four seconds? You'd have to be literally *yelling* at your prospect, "*Hey, Bill, listen to me! I'm sharp as a tack! I'm enthusiastic! I'm an expert in my field! I swear, I swear, I swear . . .*" and blah, blah, blah. You'd sound like a freaking idiot! Not to mention that, even if it all *were* true, no one would believe you anyway.

The simple fact is that the right words just don't exist. There is no combination of words that are profound enough and stealthy enough to sneak past the logic center of your prospect's mind and create an emotional reaction that goes straight to their gut; for it's there, in your prospect's gut, where first impressions get formed in fractions of a second, and they'll guide their decisions until you prove them wrong.

So if your words won't do it, then where do you turn?

The answer is simple: *your tone of voice.*

Specifically, *how you say* what you say has a profound impact on how it's perceived and, for that matter, how *you* are perceived; and not just during those all-important first four seconds, but throughout the entire conversation as well.

You see, after millions of years of evolution, the human ear has become so adept at recognizing tonal shifts that even the slightest one can have a dramatic impact on the meaning of a word or phrase. For example, when I was a kid and I did something wrong, my mom would say "*Jordan!*" in a stern, no-nonsense voice, and without her having to say another word, I immediately knew that I was in serious trouble. Conversely, if she said "*Jor-dan!*" in a singsong tone, then I immediately knew that things were fine.

On the flip side, if a sales encounter takes place in person, then a second communication modality comes into play, working hand-in-hand with tonality to help us get our point across.

We call this second modality *body language.*

Serving as the dual linchpins of an immensely powerful communication strategy known as *unconscious communication*, tonality and body language play major roles in how we get our point across—both while we're *talking* and as we're *listening.*

In essence, your tone of voice, how you move your body, the facial expressions you make, the type of smile you offer, the way you make eye contact, and all those little friendly grunts and groans you make while you're listening to someone talk—the *oohs* and *ahhs* and *ahas* and *yups*—are an integral part of human communication and have a massive impact on how you're perceived.

In terms of percentages, tonality and body language comprise approximately 90 percent of our overall communication, split evenly down the middle, with each modality having approximately a 45 percent impact, depending on which study you buy into (and there are more of them than you can count). The remaining 10 percent of communication is comprised of our *words*—meaning, the actual words we say as we verbally communicate.

That's right: only 10 percent.

Now, I know what you're probably thinking right now:

You're thinking that 10 percent sounds like *way* too low a number to measure the importance of words, *especially* in a situation when someone is trying to sell you something. In fact, if you were to think back to a time when you were being sold to, then I'm sure you would recall hanging on the salesperson's every word and judging each one based on its meaning. It was as if your logical mind was almost being *hypervigilant* as it went about deciding what level of logical certainty was most appropriate based on the logical case the salesperson had created with his words.

HUMAN COMMUNICATION

Tonality—45% +

Body Language—45% =

90%

Words—10%

So I do understand how *difficult* it can be to buy into the concept that our words aren't that important.

But here's the irony:

You've actually *misinterpreted* the meaning of my words!

You see, despite comprising only 10 percent of our communication, words aren't just important; they're actually the single most important element of our communication strategy, but—and this is a *very* big but—only when we finally open up our mouths to speak. In other words, 90 percent of the time, we're communicating without actually speaking!

Yet, still, when I walk into any phone room or I observe a sales force in the field, with the exception of maybe one or two salespeople who are blessed with perfect tonality and flawless body language, the rest of them will be completely missing the boat. In consequence, they don't get perceived as having even *close* to the level of expertise that would prompt a prospect to hand over control of the sale and let themself be *guided*.

And, *just like that*, through a process of *unwitting* self-sabotage, the sale has been poisoned from the very start, making it only a matter of time until it spirals out of control.

Yet what's even more ironic than *that* is the fact that of all the tactics and strategies that comprise the Straight Line System, tonality and body language are some of the easiest to master.

In total, of the twenty-nine tonalities that a human being uses to communicate, only *ten* of them are core-influencing tonalities—meaning that we use them over and over again as we go about influencing and persuading. Likewise, the Straight Line System has been able to consolidate the infinite number of gestures and postures and facial expressions that comprise our body language into ten core principles.

Now, for those of you who are currently saying to yourselves, "*Aha*, I *knew* there had to be a catch! Jordan made everything sound so easy, and now I find out that I have to learn twenty different things? How am I supposed to do *that*? I'm not a *kid* anymore; I'm an *adult*! And an adult can't just *learn* ten new tonalities and ten new body language principles! It's totally preposterous!"

Hopefully, that's at least a *slight* exaggeration of what you're thinking right now, but either way, if you're feeling even *remotely* like that, then I have two very important thoughts I'd like to share with you.

First, and I mean this in a kind, avuncular way:

Cut the crap! It's time for you to get out of your own way and start living the life you deserve. You are capable of becoming proficient at anything you put your mind to. All you need is an easy-to-learn, step-by-step strategy to show you the way, which is exactly what the Straight Line System is.

In fact, one of the true beauties of the Straight Line is that even after just a little bit of training, when you're still at a *very* low level of competency, you'll still get surprisingly good results.

Just how good depends on a number of variables—the industry you're in, the length of its sales cycle, how much time you dedicate to learning the system, and, of course, your skill level at the start—but most salespeople get at least a 50 percent pop in their sales over the short term—and you'll get double that if you're a complete novice who's in an industry with a very short sales cycle and lots of million-dollar producers.

In Straight Line parlance, we call this the "Good Enough Factor"—meaning that you'll still get very good results, even when you're first getting started and you've only achieved a reasonable level of proficiency.

And second, regardless of what you were thinking about having to learn all these "new" distinctions, the reality is that you don't have to actually learn *anything*. After all, implausible as it might seem, you already know everything you need to know.

In fact, not only do you already know all ten tonalities and all ten body language principles but you've also used them *countless* times throughout your life. The only difference is that, in the past, you have been using them automatically or unconsciously—without even thinking about it.

In other words, there have been countless times in your life when each one of these tonalities came out of you *naturally*, as a reaction to what you were actually feeling at the moment; and the same thing is true when it comes to body language.

Let me give you an example:

Have you ever had a time in your life when you were feeling *so* absolutely certain about something that the tonality of certainty just came flying straight out of your mouth? It was like you could literally *feel* the certainty coming through in every single word, and anyone who was listening would have had absolutely no doubt that you 100 percent believed what you were talking about.

Of course you have!

We *all* have.

And how about telling a secret? How many times in your life have you lowered your voice to *just* above a whisper to tell someone a secret?

Again, we've all done this a thousand times, because we intuitively know that a whisper *intrigues* people and *draws* them in—compelling them to listen more closely.

Now, in a sales setting, when you apply a whisper at *precisely* the right moment during a presentation, you will be shocked at the impact it has on your prospect, *especially* if you raise your voice back up right afterwards.

The key here is *modulation*.

You want to lower your voice, and then raise your voice; you want to speed up, and then slow down; you want to make a declarative statement, and then turn it into a question; you want to group certain words together, and then say others in staccato-like beats.

For instance, let's go back to the whisper, but we'll add a little *oomph* to it. Now, we have what's called a *power whisper*, which comes from deep in your gut. (Give your solar plexus a few quick pats with the palm of your right hand. That's the spot I'm referring to when I talk about your gut.) A whisper from there creates the perception that what you're saying has extra importance to it, that you *really* mean it.

It's like you're saying to the prospect, "Listen, pal, this particular point is *really* important, and it's something I really, really believe in, so you need to pay very close attention to it."

But of course, you're not actually *saying* those words. They're registering with the prospect unconsciously, in the form of a gut feeling, which moves them on an emotional level, as opposed to a logical one. You see my point?

Another great example of this is how we use enthusiasm to create *massive* emotional certainty in our prospect—meaning, they get an overwhelming sense that whatever product we're selling simply *must* be good.

To be clear, though, what I'm *not* talking about is that crazy brand of over-the-top enthusiasm, where you're yelling and screaming and flailing your arms about, as you go on and on about how amazing your product is. Not only is that completely ridiculous, but it's also the easiest way to get your client running towards the exit.

I'm talking about something called *bottled enthusiasm*, which sits just below the surface and literally *bubbles* over as you speak. It's about enunciating your words with absolute *clarity* and stressing your consonants so that your words have *intensity* to them. It's like you're talking with your fists clenched, and there's an active volcano inside you ready to erupt at any second—but of course it doesn't, because you're an expert who's in total control.

That sort of bottled enthusiasm makes a massive impact on someone emotionally, and it's one of the earmarks of sounding like an expert. Just always remember to never stay in any one tonality for too long, or else the prospect will become bored—or in scientific terms, *habituate*—and ultimately tune out.

To that end, I am constantly using my tonality and body language to insure against that. You see, tuning out does not happen randomly; it's based on a conscious equation the prospect is running as to whether or not you're a person worth listening to. Prospects ask themselves: Can this person help me achieve my goals? Can this person help me get what I want in life? Can this person help me resolve the pain I have?

If the answer to those questions is *no,* then they tune out; if the answer is yes, they listen. It's as simple as that.

That's why it's so absolutely crucial, right out of the *gate,* to come off as being sharp as a tack, enthusiastic as hell, and an expert in your field. If you *do,* then not only will you keep your prospect hanging on your every word, but they'll also let you take control of the sale and begin the process of moving them down the Straight Line.

Now, in terms of how to start using this in the real world, you'll find that with just a little bit of practice, you'll be applying the right tonality and body language *unconsciously*—meaning, *automatically*—whenever you find yourself in a situation of influence. But, until then, you need to be extra vigilant about *consciously* applying the right tonality and body language to every word and every turn of phrase. This will ensure that your prospect stays firmly in your magnetic zone and doesn't tune out.

– – – – – – – – – –

R

⸻⸻⸻⸻⸻

– – – – – – – – – –

Rapport on a conscious & unconscious level

Before we move on to the next chapter, I want to go through some key nuances regarding the relationship between the *conscious* mind and the *unconscious* mind—specifically, how they work hand in hand with one another to guide all your prospect's decisions, *especially* during those crucial opening seconds, when your ability to bypass their conscious mind and speak directly to their unconscious mind will dictate whether you succeed or fail at taking control of the sale, and then again at the end of the sale, when your ability to speak to both minds at once will allow you to push past the action threshold of even the toughest prospects and achieve the highest level of Straight Line competency, which means that you can close anyone who's closable.

So, that being said, let me start by dispelling one of the greatest myths regarding the relationship between the two minds, which is: that the *conscious* mind is the more powerful of the two.

Nothing could be further from the truth.

Some 200 million times more powerful than its *conscious* counterpart, your *unconscious* mind, with its blazing speed and near infinite storage capacity, is what keeps you alive as you move through the world. Working *around* the clock, it controls your entire autonomic nervous system— regulating your heartbeat, your blood pressure, your respiration, your digestion, your hormone secretions, and every other system in your body that seems to hum along effortlessly without you having to think about it.

Broadly speaking, the primary goal of your unconscious mind is to keep things the same, or, in scientific terms, maintain a state of homeostasis. Your weight, your body temperature, your blood sugar level, the amount of oxygen in your blood, the amount of light hitting your retinas; each of these things and countless others like them are constantly being adjusted to maintain a certain set point that a million years of evolution has deemed to be optimal.

Conversely, your conscious mind is literally *starving* for process- ing power as it tries to make sense of things while you move through the world. In consequence, at any given moment, it can only focus on 3 or 4 percent of the surrounding environment, and it deletes the rest—allowing it to focus 100 percent of its relatively meager processing power on a few key items that it deems most important. Collectively, these key items represent conscious awareness, and the way you analyze them is through logic and reason.

For example, at this very moment, 95 percent of your conscious mind is dedicated to your primary focus, which is reading the words I've written, and listening to your own inner monologue as it debates what you've just read. The remainder is dedicated to your secondary focus, which consists of a handful of things that are happening close enough to you to be picked up by one of your five senses, and are either too extreme or too intermittent for your conscious mind to become desensitized to them and block them out—a blaring TV in the background, a noxious odor, the banging and clanging from a nearby construction site, someone snoring, your own breathing if you have a stuffy nose.

Meanwhile, the 96 or 97 percent of the world that the conscious mind is deleting is being captured in its entirety by the unconscious mind. You see, not only is it responsible for regulating all your bodily functions, it also acts as the central depository for all your memories.

In essence, everything you've seen or heard has been neatly filed away there, no matter how insignificant it may have seemed at the time or whether you remember it now or not. Your unconscious mind recorded the experience, compared and contrasted it with similar past experiences, and then used the results to refine and augment your internal "map of the world," as the phrase goes, which serves as your internal barometer for formulating snap decisions, instant judgments, and first impressions, your internal model of how you perceive your environment, how you believe it should operate, and how you believe you should operate within it, which types of behaviors lie inside your comfort zone and which ones don't.

Then, to help you *navigate* the map—and to ensure that your snap decisions, instant judgments, and first impressions remain consistent with the beliefs in your map—your unconscious mind also creates "patterns of behavior," allowing you to instantly respond to situations that have been previously "mapped out," in a way that's fluid and elegant, consistent with your beliefs about yourself and the world, and that requires no conscious thought whatsoever.

In essence, this three-step process of generalization, map-making, and the creation of patterns is what allows you to move through an unfamiliar environment without having to treat everything you see as if it were the first time you've seen it.

For example, when you walk up to a strange door, you don't have to pause and examine each one of its features and wonder if it's safe to turn the little round knob that's sticking out on one side. Despite never having seen this particular door before, your unconscious mind has been through this scenario countless times, so it springs into action the instant the door comes into your field of vision—working at near light speed to match this particular door to the spot on your map marked "Doors" and the various strategies for safely entering and exiting them, in non-combat situations and where no new construction is taking place.

Now, obviously I'm taking a bit of poetic license here, but my point is spot-on: rather than having to stop at every new door or every fresh crack in the sidewalk or countless other occurrences, so your conscious mind can *logic* things out, your unconscious mind takes immediate action and saves your conscious mind the trouble.

In fact, from your *conscious* mind's perspective, these snap judgments and instant decisions are based on *gut feelings*, and it will act in accordance with them until they're proven wrong.

This happens frequently in sales, and when it does happen, it's almost always the result of something foolish or off-base that the salesman said. In other words, while your prospect's first impression of you was a result of your unconscious communication, it can be completely destroyed by a few choice words; and that makes perfect sense, considering that words are the building blocks for airtight logical cases, which then serve as the basis for our conscious decisions.

However, when it comes to airtight *emotional* cases, we rely far more heavily on *unconscious* communication, in the form of tonality and body language, than on the words others say.

When the sales encounter is over the phone, we'll use our ten core tonalities to move our prospect emotionally, while the words they're attached to will move the prospect logically; and when the encounter is in person, we'll also use body language to move our prospect emotionally, while our *words* will continue to move them logically.

So, at the end of the day, whether it's in person or over the phone, the strategies you employ and the outcomes you desire will always be the same: you'll use words to influence your prospect's conscious mind, and tonality and body language to influence their unconscious mind. And the outcome of the former will be an airtight *logical* case, and the outcome of the latter will be airtight *emotional* case. All you need to know is precisely what words to say and when to say them, and what unconscious communication to apply and when to apply it. It's as simple and straightforward as that.

Insofar as what *words* you're going to use to accomplish this task, I'm going to be handing them to you on a silver platter in Chapter 11, in the form of a *foolproof* scriptwriting formula that you can apply to any business or industry with massive success.

However, as foolproof as this formula is, your success is still going to be contingent on your ability to trigger a *key* emotional state within yourself as you're about to enter the sales encounter, and then maintain that state to the very end.

We refer to this process as *state management*, and it's one of the most important elements in achieving success.

In the following chapter, I'm going to take you for a trip down memory lane—back to the early days of Stratton, to show you the true power of state management when it comes to sales, and then provide you with a paint-by-number strategy for managing your own state that is not only wildly effective but also extremely easy to use.

5

STATE MANAGEMENT

BEFORE THINGS AT STRATTON HAD SPIRALED OUT OF CONTROL, the boardroom had been a truly remarkable place. It was an egalitarian society in the purest sense of the phrase, a meritocracy where you were judged solely on your performance, not by the weight of your diploma or your family connections. Once you entered the boardroom, it no longer mattered who you were, where you came from, or what mistakes you'd made in the past. All of that could be left behind.

In essence, the Straight Line System served as the Great Equalizer, allowing even the most disempowered men and women to completely reinvent themselves and start their lives anew.

To give you an idea of just how massive an impact the Straight Line System had on these kids, I would only be *slightly* exaggerating if I said that more than half of them showed up at my door with only a borderline ability to walk and chew gum at the same time. Then, sixty days later, I'd see the same kid and—*bam!*—that kid would be completely transformed.

No matter how many times I witnessed it, this radical transformation was never lost on me. Everything from how they walked to how they talked to how they dressed to how they shook hands to the way they made eye contact; you could literally *feel* the confidence oozing off them.

Now, for those of you who are currently saying to yourself: "I don't see what the big deal is. I mean, if you paid *me* fifty thousand dollars a month when *I* was in my twenties, I would've changed anything you wanted me to. I'd have walked differently, I'd have talked differently, I'd have dressed differently, and I'd even have washed behind my ears if that's what it took! I mean, who wouldn't, right?"

If you were thinking anything along those lines, I can't say that I really fault you. After all, your argument is both intelligent *and* well thought out, and shows a very solid grasp on human nature. Unfortunately, that doesn't change the fact you're completely barking up the wrong tree!

You see, the Stratton training program was six months long, so at the time I witnessed their transformation, none of the kids had started making any money yet. They were all still trainees, which meant they were still flat broke!

So what was it then? What caused this transformation?

In truth, there was more than one thing behind it, but at the heart of the transformation was a powerful visualization technique that I taught the Strattonites called *future pacing*.

In short, future pacing entails running an imaginary movie through your mind where you get to see yourself in the future having already achieved a certain outcome. The *result* is that you get to experience the positive *feelings* associated with a future achievement *right now*, as opposed to having to wait until a few years from now, when you actually achieve it.

During my daily sales meetings, I always made it a point to remind the trainees of the importance of future pacing their own success, and I also made them run the positive movie right there in their seats, allowing them to *see* themselves in the future already being rich and living the Life. And, of course, in the same way that I told the first twelve Strattonites to "act as if," I kept repeating that message to the boardroom again and again and again.

I would say, "Act as if you're a wealthy man, rich already, and you will become rich. Act as if you have unmatched confidence, and people will have confidence in you. Act as if you have all the answers, and the answers will come to you."

In other words, I told them that they should not only think like wealthy people but to also carry themselves that way, because it leads to the right state of mind.

As previously mentioned, the technical term for this is *state management.*

In essence, when you're managing your emotional state, you're *temporarily* blocking out any troubling thoughts or emotions that might normally make you feel negative—thereby allowing yourself to maintain a positive state of mind.

What makes state management so important in achieving success is that your current emotional state determines whether or not you'll be able to access your internal resources at that moment to achieve your outcome.

When you're in an *empowered* state—like "certainty," for instance—then you're able to access your internal resources, which then sets you up for massive success. Conversely, when you're in a *disempowered* state, you're *blocked* from accessing your internal resources, and you've set yourself up for massive failure.

It's very similar to how a valve works.

An *empowered* state is the equivalent of the valve to your internal resources being fully open, allowing you to access them at will, while a *disempowered* state is the equivalent of the valve being closed, *blocking* you from accessing your resources, no matter how badly you might need them. Let me give you an example:

Imagine that you have some of the *best* sales skills in the world. You're an expert at every aspect of the Straight Line System—from taking immediate control of the sale to running world-class looping patterns and closing the deal.

But let's say you walk through your prospect's door in a state of absolute *uncertainty*, then how good of a salesperson can you be at that moment?

Not very good, right?

You see, at that particular moment, you're blocked from accessing your internal resources—in this case, your sales skills—so no matter how great of a salesperson you *could* be, you're simply unable to access that greatness.

The same thing goes with your personal life.

Let's say you're a parent.

Now, obviously, you love your kids to death, and you pride yourself on being an amazing parent. In fact, you've even read a few books on parenting, to give you strategy and insight, so you really know what you're doing. But let's say you come home after a *really* tough day at work, and you walk in the door in a state of *anger and impatience*—two very disempowering states—then how good of a parent can you be at that moment?

Again, not very good.

Your anger and impatience have blocked you from accessing your resources for parenting. So, despite the fact that you still love your kids just as much as usual, and despite the fact that you still possess all those wonderful skills for being an amazing parent, at *that* particular moment you're blocked from accessing them.

Here's the bottom line:

As a salesperson—or as *any* success-oriented person—you must learn how to start triggering the key empowered states; otherwise, you set yourself up for a lifetime of pain. There are no two ways about it.

However, one point I want to clarify here is that what I am *not* saying is that you need to, or for that matter should even *want* to, live in empowered states *all* the time. That's completely nuts!

Just think that through for a second:

I mean, what do you call someone who walks around all day long with their chest puffed out, in a state of absolute certainty?

You call him an *asshole*, right? We *hate* those people!

And you don't want to be one!

I don't want to belabor the point, but this is a far bigger problem in the self-development world than you'd think, especially with people who attend seminars that focus solely on inner-game skills. The problem that arises is that when you teach those skills without the context of a real-world application, the attendees almost invariably get the wrong message.

The key distinction here is that once you've learned the technique for *triggering* an empowered state (I'm going to teach you the most powerful one in the world in a moment), you only want to use it at certain key moments, when it matters most, like before you enter a sales encounter, or try to close a business deal, or enter into a negotiation, or even if it's just an important decision you need to make in your personal life.

In fact, in the latter case, you *definitely* want to make sure that you're in an empowered state, because human beings, as a species, make their worst personal decisions when they're in a disempowered state (and their best decisions when they're in an empowered state).

In terms of achieving success in sales, there are four key states that you need to learn how to trigger at will within state management. We call them the four Cs:

Certainty, clarity, confidence, and courage.

These are your linchpin states for achieving wealth and success. If you don't learn how to trigger them, then you're playing Russian roulette with your future—essentially *hoping* that you'll be in the right state when you enter a sales encounter, versus *knowing* you will be because you have a surefire strategy to do it. The name of that strategy is *olfactory anchoring*.

I created olfactory anchoring almost a decade ago, in response to my personal need to instantly trigger an empowered state under what were becoming increasingly odd circumstances.

As the story goes, when I was on my first global speaking tour, I began to find myself in situations where it was crucial for me to be in an empowered state despite the fact that the surrounding environment was often working heavily against me.

For example, I was constantly getting cornered into doing last-second TV interviews, talk shows, radio shows, newspaper interviews, sponsor requests, and photo opportunities, all of which required that I look my best, act my best, and, in fact, *be* my best at all times. No matter how tired, jet-lagged, or completely burned out I was from being on a multiyear speaking tour, I was expected to *perform*, plain and simple.

In addition, on those very same days, I would also have to get up on stage and give anywhere from a two- to a ten-hour talk to as many as twelve thousand people who had paid good money to see me, so the moment I hit that stage, I had to take my state from zero to 100 mph in a matter of seconds.

That was the reality I was facing.

At the time, I had just started using a state management technique called *NLP anchoring*, which was part of a group of techniques and strategies that make up a body of knowledge known as neuro-linguistic programming, or NLP, for short.

Operating on the fringe of mainstream psychology, NLP's basic premise is that the human brain functions similarly to a computer and hence can be *programmed* as such to make near instant changes to certain key behavioral patterns. The only sticking point, however, is that before you can make any changes, you need to know two important things first:

- **How to write code for the human brain**

- **What type of software to embed the code in**

It sounds complicated, I know, but in reality it's the exact opposite. Let me explain, and you'll see exactly what I mean.

According to NLP, the software of the brain is language, and the way you write code is by creating language *patterns*, which consist of a group of words—as brief as a short sentence or as long as a few paragraphs—that have been structured in accordance with a series of basic yet extremely powerful linguistic principles that can be used to reprogram virtually any person's brain, including your own, in a number of very profound ways.

One of those ways forms the basis of NLP anchoring.

The basic premise of NLP anchoring is that human beings have the ability to *choose* how they feel at a particular moment in time, as opposed to it being chosen *for* them by what's going on in their surrounding environment or their personal life.

In other words, we can be *proactive* when it comes to choosing our emotional state, as opposed to *reactive*, which is what most human beings have been conditioned to think is our only choice.

A vast majority of human beings believe that their current emotional state is a result of outside forces that are being exerted on *them*. For example, if positive things are happening to you, then you'll end up falling into a positive emotional state; and if *negative* things are happening to you, then you'll end up in a *negative* emotional state.

Now, obviously, the proactive nature of NLP's state philosophy is attractive to anyone in sales, and for that matter anyone who wants to live a more empowered life. To that end, NLP has distilled the entire state management process into two core elements, both of which are under a person's conscious control. The first of these two elements is:

What you choose to focus on.

In essence, at any particular moment, you have the ability to choose the precise direction of your focus; and *based* on that choice, you'll fall into a state that's congruent with what you've chosen to focus on.

For example, if you spend the next few minutes focusing on everything that's great in your life—a recent business success, being in a loving relationship, the health of your children, a recent goal you achieved, a family getaway—then you'll quickly pop into a positive, empowered state that reflects all those wonderful things.

Conversely, if you spend the same amount of time focusing on everything that's *wrong* in your life—a recent business failure, a divorce, a sick child, a recent goal you failed to achieve—then you'll quickly fall into a *disempowered* state that reflects all those crappy things. It's as simple as that.

The second of these two elements is:

Y*our current physiology.*

Comprised of the sum of all the possible ways that you can move and hold your body—your posture, your facial expressions, how you move your appendages, your rate of breathing, your overall level of motion—physiology of human beings as it relates to each emotional state is nearly identical across all cultures.

In other words, human beings, as a species, will all adapt virtually the same physiology when they're in a happy, positive emotional state. Put another way, people who were born and raised in Papua New Guinea don't smile when they're depressed or frown when they're happy any more than Eskimos do, or people who were raised in Portugal do.

For example, if I pointed to a closed door and said to you: "Behind that door is a very happy woman! For a prize of ten thousand dollars, I want you to tell me which of each pair of these physical traits best describes her: Is she smiling or is she frowning? Is her head held high or is her head slumped over? Is she breathing fully and deeply, or is her breathing slow and shallow? Are her shoulders pulled back, or are they rolled slightly forward? Is she standing up straight, or is she slightly hunched over? Are her eyes opened wide or are they slightly narrowed?" (And, of course, the same questions would apply if it were a depressed woman.)

Now, just so you know, I've asked both of those versions to live audiences all over the world—the US, the UK, Australia, South Africa, China, Russia, Singapore, Malaysia, Mexico, Canada, Iceland, Germany, and pretty much anywhere else you can think of—and no matter where I've been in the world, the entire audience always answers these questions in the same exact way.

In other words, we know what a *depressed* person looks like and we know what a *happy* person looks like; and we also know what an angry person looks like and what a loving person looks like too; and we all know what an impatient person looks like and we know what a calm person looks like. It's all very logical.

Now, let me ask you another state management question, albeit from a slightly different angle. Let's say you were in a depressed state right now, and I offered you $50,000 to act happy for the next sixty seconds. Could you do it?

Yes, of *course* you could!

It would be as simple as consciously making certain obvious changes to your physiology, ones that you had used countless times in your life, since you were a little boy or girl.

However, what if I offered you $100,000—no, make that

$1 million—and asked you to make the same changes to your physiology as last time, albeit with one important difference: *this time*, I need you to maintain a happy physiology for the next eighteen hours straight. Could you do it?

No way.

No matter how hard you tried, you simply couldn't pull it off.

It's impossible.

To be clear, this has nothing to do with you being weak or strong or anything of the sort. It's simply the way human beings are built, as a species.

You see, while it's true that we can, in fact, make ourselves feel any way we want at any given moment, that moment is fleeting—giving us a window of opportunity that's anywhere from five minutes to maybe an hour at most. After that, you'll slowly start to settle back to whatever state you were in before.

Now, if any of this stuff still seems foreign to you, here's a quick exercise that will really clear things up. Ready?

Okay, I want you to think back to *all* the times in your life when someone asked you to manage your state, and you actually *did*, but you called it something else at the time.

For instance:

How many times has someone said to you: "Keep your chin up!" or "Put on a brave face!" or "Look alert!" or "Keep cool!" or "Smile and act polite!" or "Don't lose your temper!"

See my point?

The reality is that we've *all* tried to manage our state at various times in our life, and sometimes we were successful and sometimes not. The goal of anchoring is to eliminate the "not."

So, with that, let's get specific.

NLP's first leap of logic was based on the idea that human beings could proactively manage their emotional state with near 100 percent success by directing their focus and their physiology in a specific way.

The second leap of logic was to combine this concept with classic Pavlovian conditioning, as in: Pavlov's dogs.

Remember Pavlov's dogs?

As the story goes, sometime around the turn of the last century, a little-known Russian scientist named Ivan Pavlov conducted an experiment involving a starving dog (very common, at the time), a juicy piece of meat (almost impossible to find, at the time), and an extremely loud bell (very common, one would think, although who really knows).

Either way, the experiment's protocol was simple:

Present the starving dog with the juicy piece of meat, while simultaneously ringing a bell. This he did.

Not surprisingly, the dog instantly began to salivate at the sight of the meat, while the sound of the bell was merely coincidental to him, at least at first. However, what Pavlov quickly noticed was that as he kept repeating this process over and over again, it didn't take long until the dog would start to salivate *just* from the sound of the bell. The sight of the meat was no longer necessary.

The reason for this, Pavlov concluded, was that each time he repeated the experiment, the dog's brain would develop a stronger link between the sound of the bell and the sight of the meat, until, finally, the link had grown so strong that the mere act of ringing the bell would be powerful enough to trigger salivation.

In NLP, the ringing sound of the bell is referred to as an *anchor*, the act of *ringing* the bell is referred to as *firing off an anchor*, and the process by which two formally unrelated items become linked together in this way is referred to as *setting an anchor*.

The most common state that salespeople will try to set an anchor for is a state of absolute certainty, and the most common anchor they'll choose to try to link it to is a combination of shouting the word "yes" and simultaneously clapping their hands.

Now, if you're thinking that screaming the word "yes" while executing a single clap of your hands doesn't seem quite as intense as tempting a starving dog with a piece of juicy beef (while ringing a bell that's loud enough to wake the dead), then you're in the same boat that I was: feeling frustrated, skeptical, but still hopeful for an answer.

Yet, on the flip side, I knew that the *science* behind NLP's approach was sound, and that the payoff for cracking the code would be incalculable—not so much to me, but to the tens of millions of people who would be attending my live events over the next few years.

You see, unlike most people, I was blessed with a natural ability to manage my state at an extremely high level, so anchoring was really more of a luxury to me than a necessity.

Unfortunately, though, for every oddball out there like me, there are ten million *normal* folks whose natural abilities in this area lie on the opposite end of the spectrum. In consequence, I continued to experiment with a number of different strategies that could be combined with basic NLP anchoring in order to ratchet up its effectiveness. It took just a bit over a month, until I finally struck gold.

In the summer of 2009, I gave birth to a wildly effective state management technique that I proudly named *olfactory anchoring*. She was born weighing just over an ounce, and was just under two inches long. She was on the thin side, for sure, but perfectly symmetrical nonetheless. However, out of all her defining features, there was one in particular that stood out above the rest:

She stunk!

6

A SUREFIRE FORMULA FOR MANAGING YOUR STATE

FOR THE RECORD, I CONSIDER MY DISCOVERY OF OLFACTORY anchoring to be one of those fortunate situations where I was able to stand on the shoulders of a genius.

The genius to whom I'm referring is Dr. Richard Bandler, the brilliant and wildly enigmatic scientist, visionary, entertainer, and hypnotist extraordinaire who invented NLP, in conjunction with linguistics professor John Grinder.

Focusing on inner-world distinctions such as belief systems, value hierarchies, and state management, NLP took the self-development world by storm in the early eighties and has played a central role in fueling the industry's growth ever since.

The reason I began studying it was a desire to learn two specific strategies that NLP was particularly well known for at the time. The first strategy was a *timeline regression*, which was designed to help people crack the code of their limiting beliefs and replace them with empowering beliefs; and the second strategy was *anchoring*, which, as discussed in the previous chapter, was designed to help people trigger a peak emotional state at will.

In the end, while I had tremendous success at implementing the former, but the latter, as I explained, had come up seriously short. So it was that, in the summer of 2009, I began testing various ways to enhance anchoring's effectiveness.

In early 2010, I struck gold.

In retrospect, I'm still not sure why it took me so long to crack the code for anchoring. After all, the difference between NLP anchoring and olfactory anchoring is only two strategies I added, each of which addresses one of the two crucial aspects of anchoring that Bandler considered especially vulnerable to being poorly executed.

The first vulnerability had to do with how intense you were able to get your state to at the precise moment when you introduced the anchor. The key, Bandler explained, is that you have to be at the absolute *tippy-top* of the state, in terms of the emotional intensity you feel inside, in order to successfully set an anchor. Anything less than that, and the anchor won't set.

In terms of how this would relate to the certainty scale from Chapter 1, you'd have to be at an absolute, unequivocal 10, with no ifs, ands, or buts; only then, at that precise moment, when you felt the certainty literally *bubbling up* inside you, like a *seething* volcano, could you introduce an anchor and truly set it.

So that's the first aspect of NLP anchoring that tends to trip people up: the difficulty of trying to artificially get yourself into a state of absolute certainty or, for that matter, absolute *anything*, as opposed to being there organically.

The *second* vulnerability had to do with the *type* of anchor you choose (the equivalent of the bell in Pavlov's experiment).

As Bandler explained, not only does the anchor need to hit you all at once but it also needs to stand out in a dramatic way. A common, everyday sound or gesture simply won't cut it. It needs to be *extreme*—the more extreme the better, in fact—and the more unusual the better too. In essence, you want to use something that's going to hit your brain in an unforgettable way and literally *shock* your senses. That's what a great anchor does, and it's absolutely crucial that you have one. But don't waste any of *your* time trying to find one. A little over seven years ago, I stumbled upon the world's greatest anchor, and I'm going to be handing it to you on a silver platter in this very chapter.

Now, in terms of the best way to *teach* you olfactory anchoring, what I've found, over the years, is that the secret is to take you through NLP anchoring first. This provides you with the perfect context for truly mastering olfactory anchoring, which, by the way, is so easy to master that not only will you be able to do it in one sitting but a seven-year-old could do it as well.

So, with that, let's get to it.

There are five basic steps to NLP anchoring:

Step #1: Choose a state

This is where you set an intention for the emotional state you want to anchor. This will always be a conscious decision, based on the circumstances that you're *about* to face, not what you're currently facing. In other words, anchoring is a forward-looking process that's proactive in nature.

For the purpose of this exercise, let's choose a state of *absolute certainty*, as this is the state that you *must* be in when you enter any sales encounter.

Step #2: Choose your focus

This is where you close your eyes and go back to a moment in your life when you were feeling absolutely, positively certain. A perfect example of this would be the moment after you *just* closed a *really* tough sale, as a result of sounding totally *awesome*. For whatever reason, you were at your very best that day, and now, as you bask in the sale's afterglow, you have that superconfident feeling—that feeling of absolute certainty where you know you can take on the world and close anyone who's closable.

Once you've located that memory, I want you to create a vivid picture of it in your mind's eye. I want you to take in the whole scene, so you can see all the players who were there, looking *just* the way they looked, including how they were dressed, how their hair was styled, and even how the room looked.

Creating an internal picture like this, where you're looking down at yourself from above, involves being in what is called a disassociated state, and it's a crucial aspect of goal-setting and self-motivation—inasmuch as it allows you to see yourself completing a certain goal or task or an even more complete vision for your future. However, for the purposes of setting an anchor, there's an even *more* powerful way to use this internal picture, which I'll get to in a few moments, in step four.

Step #3: Choose your physiology

This is where you're going to change your physiology to match the *exact* physiology of the state that you're trying to anchor. For example, in this case, you're going to make sure that you're *standing* certain and holding your head certain and walking certain and talking certain and even *breathing* certain, so that literally *every* aspect of your body, including your most *minute* gestures and facial expressions, is resonating with the emotion of absolute certainty.

If you think it'll help, you can even take the picture from step two and actually put it in motion, so you're now seeing yourself in a movie, and you can use that as your model as you adopt the physiology of absolute certainty.

Remember, being shy or bashful with your physiology is not going to serve you at this point. Quite simply, this is one of those cases where *more* is more, not *less* is more, and that goes for your focus too, as you're about to see right now, in step four.

Step #4: Intensify your state

This step involves using your five sensory modalities—also known as your *five senses*—to take the picture you've created in your mind's eye in step two and use your brain to manipulate it in a way that intensifies the feeling of absolute certainty that it creates inside of you.

First let me take you through the five sensory modalities, which are:

Visual: this is what you see, both externally, in the real world, and internally, in your mind's eye. In the latter case, the picture can be from a memory, or it can be something that you've created yourself using your imagination, or it can be a combination of the two.

Auditory: this is what you hear, both externally and internally, and with the same permutations as above.

Kinesthetic: this is what you feel, both externally and internally, and with the same permutations as above.

Gustatory: this is what you taste, both externally and internally, and with the same permutations as above.

Olfactory: this is what you smell, both externally and internally, and with the same permutations as above.

Now, for the most part, we tend to rely on the first three modalities to make sense of the world, with our visual modality being the most dominant, followed by our auditory and kinesthetic modalities, respectively. But, of course, when you're dealing with the brain, nothing is set in stone. For example, if you're a chef, then you'll rely heavily on your *gustatory* modality, and if you're a wine taster or perfumer, then you'll rely heavily on your olfactory modality.

As I explained above, the way to use these modalities in anchoring is to take the picture in your mind's eye and alter it so it becomes more powerful to you emotionally.

For example, if you focus on the image right now, in your mind's eye, you can instruct your brain to make the picture bigger, and brighter, and sharper, and you can even move it closer to you; and doing that will tend to amplify whatever feeling the picture gives you, which, in this particular case, is a feeling of absolute certainty. However, as it is in real life, there's only so far that a still picture can take you, which is why the feelings that we get from watching a movie or a TV show are far more intense than the feelings we get from looking through a stack of pictures or from flipping through a magazine.

In fact, the evolution of the motion picture business serves as a perfect metaphor for the relationship between the size and the quality of the images we see and the emotions that we feel as a result of them. For example, the industry started with silent movies shot in black-and-white, which were replaced by talking pictures shot in black-and-white, which were replaced by movies shot in color, which were replaced by movies shot in Technicolor and stereo, which were replaced by movies shot in wide screen and Technicolor with stereo and Dolby sound reduction, all the way to IMAX theaters, with 3-D and surround sound and so forth.

Notice the obvious trend towards making things bigger and brighter and clearer and more realistic . . . until they hit a certain point and the trend began to reverse itself, with things like super-tall IMAX screens, 3-D, and the shaking seats of Sensurround never really catching on, despite their providing a more "lifelike" experience.

You see, this is exactly how we use the five sensory modalities to intensify our state of certainty—by taking the image you've created in your mind's eye and putting it through the same evolutionary process as the motion picture industry. I'll guide you through it right now.

PUTTING YOUR BRAIN TO WORK

I want you to start by taking the still picture you created in your mind's eye and putting it into motion, so you can actually see yourself moving in the picture, and being your best self, as you go about closing this huge sale. If it helps, you can even put a frame around the picture and imagine that it's a flat-screen TV.

The point is that by turning a still picture into a *motion* picture, you'll start feeling more connected to the scene and your state of certainty will start to intensify—especially when we execute our next step, which is to add on dialog from your memory. So, do that right now: add on the appropriate dialog, as best as you can remember, and give yourself that same, perfect tonality and body language. Or, if the dialog you recall doesn't suit you, you can create new dialog—choosing words that will empower you and help you trigger the exact state you want.

Now it's time to make your movie bigger and brighter and clearer and move it closer to you, and even add on 3-D or any other change— but, remember, each change should make the movie seem more *real* to you and, hence, increase your level of certainty; so if you reach a point of diminishing returns with any of your changes (like when you are forced to sit in the front row of a theater or when you turn up the brightness on your TV too much or the volume is too loud), slowly reverse the change until you hit the exact sweet spot with each aspect of the movie.

As you're making these various "edits" to this internal movie, notice how the feelings *associated* with this memory continue to intensify and intensify. And then you can intensify those feelings even further by imagining them occupying a certain part of your body, like just over your heart or your solar plexus, and then placing the palm of your hand over that spot and noticing how the feeling tends to spin or tumble in a certain direction. Then allow your hand to move with that feeling, until they merge into one entity. You can use your hand to spin the feeling even faster, and you can even infuse your favorite color into the feeling, or have little explosions of fireworks shooting out if it . . . And, with that, let's pause for a moment.

I have a quick question for you:

Are you thinking that I've lost my mind a bit? I mean, feelings that tumble and spin and have colors and fireworks shooting out of them? There's no denying that it sounds a little bit *wacky*, don't you think? In fact, I'm the first one to admit it! But here's the thing: do you think I would really waste your time and mine going through all this when I have more than enough other things to write more directly about than just the Straight Line System, which I invented?

All these little adjustments you make, using the power of your mind, will, in fact, intensify your state even further, which is crucial, because you can only set an anchor when you're at the absolute pinnacle of a state! (This strategy alone won't get you there, but it sets you up for olfactory anchoring in a very big way.)

Step #5: Set your anchor

Now we're at step five, which is where you actually *set your anchor*. What this entails is taking the intense state that you've just created and linking it to a word or mantra, or to some external sound or sharp feeling, like clapping your hands and screaming the word "yes"—which was when the entire process had begun to break down for me.

It started with my struggle to find a sound or a word or a movement that felt extreme enough and unique enough to serve as an anchor that I could fire in any situation. For whatever reason, nothing felt *right*, nothing felt *profound*—until, one day, it did.

Just how I came up with the idea to use sense of smell I don't fully recall, although it definitely had something to do with my memories from childhood. You see, as an adult, it never ceased to amaze me how even the slightest whiff of something that I had smelled during my childhood—a freshly cut grass field in the Catskill Mountains during summer camp, low tide at the jetty where my dad took me fishing, or the musky, mothballed scent of my grandma's house—was enough to send the most powerful memories rushing back, to the point where they viscerally hit me.

Once I hit upon the idea of using the sense of smell to set an anchor, it didn't take long to find the perfect product. There were two requirements:

1 **It had to be a scent that was extreme enough, unusual enough, powerful enough, and pungent enough to meet Bandler's criteria, yet still be pleasing enough to the nose to not gross me out or become its own negative anchor.**

2 **It had to have an unobtrusive delivery system that was portable, practical, and personal to me—meaning, I could easily slip it into my pocket, remove it without fanfare, and then use it to fire off my anchor without the scent escaping into my surroundings and impacting the people around me.**

The name of the product I found was BoomBoom. See what this is at www.boomboomenergy.com.

BoomBoom came in a sleek black tube about the size of a ChapStick, so all I had to do was unscrew the top, give myself a blast up each nostril, and, *just like that*, I popped into my ideal state.

It was an amazing breakthrough for sure, although the breakthrough it *paved the way* for was considerably more amazing, and what truly turned olfactory anchoring into the foolproof state management strategy that it is today.

So what was this second breakthrough?

Well, simply put, I figured out a *laughably* simple way to eliminate steps two, three, and four from NLP's five-step anchoring process, leaving behind a leaner, meaner, and infinitely more user-friendly two-step process that I officially dubbed *olfactory anchoring*—because of the odorous centerpiece on which its foundation was built, namely BoomBoom.

To explain exactly how I did it, let me go back a step:

After I became a master practitioner in NLP, I spent the next six months trying to set an anchor for myself for a state of *certainty*. But, no matter how many times I tried, when I got to step four—which was using the five modalities to intensify my focus—things began to break down.

The problems started with the memory I chose to focus on. I figured what moment in my life had I ever been more absolutely certain than on that magical Tuesday evening when I first drew the Straight Line on my trusty whiteboard? I'm talking about the moment I described in detail in Chapter 2, where my window of clarity opened. I couldn't think of a time when I felt more absolutely certain about anything.

But, to my own shock, when I tried to set an anchor, it didn't take. No anchor was set. So I tried again, and again, and again.

Nothing. No result.

So I tried focusing on different memories—older memories, newer memories, recent memories, memories where I was selling, memories where I was training salespeople, memories when I was speaking onstage—but no matter how *powerful* the memories were, and no matter how many times I tried to use the five sensory modalities to get to the absolute *pinnacle* of the state, in my heart of hearts I knew I hadn't gotten there.

The necessity of having to be at the absolute peak of a state in order to successfully set an anchor makes this strategy extraordinarily tough to execute. Whether you have someone guiding you through the process or not, to actually manufacture an artificial state of *absolute certainty*—I mean, to *truly-truly* do this, with no bullshit or exaggeration—is a major long shot, and most importantly, it's also prone to massive self-delusion, where people try to *talk* themselves into having succeeded because they desperately want the benefit.

In fact, when it comes to setting an anchor with NLP, I've seen more of that well-meaning self-delusion than anything, especially at live events, where people feel compelled to go along with the crowd, so they jump up and down and cheer and clap their hands and scream the word "yes" like wild banshees, and then high-five each other over the "successful" anchor they've just set.

The stark reality, however, is that the numerous benefits they're getting from being in an elevated state—they'll learn faster, they'll remember more, they'll have an *experience* that they'll never forget (and that they'll buy tickets for again!)—are only temporary.

So where am I going with all this?

Well, in the end, what I eventually came to realize was that the only *surefire* way for me to be truly at that ultra-intense level of *absolute certainty* that's required to set a legitimate anchor was to wait until I was actually in that state organically and set my anchor then.

In other words, why try to manufacture an ultrapeak state of absolute certainty through a series of powerful yet entirely subjective NLP techniques and never really know if I ever got there? All I had to do was wait until I closed a really big sale, in the real world, which caused me to pop me into a peak state of absolute certainty organically, and then, *right then*—and I mean *right then*, in that very instant—when I was basking in the afterglow of closing an awesome sale, and I knew in every cell of my body that I *truly* was in an *organic* state of *absolute certainty*, as opposed to an artificially manufactured imitation, I would bring out my BoomBoom and take a giant whiff up each nostril —*boom! boom!*— and just like that, I'd have set myself one powerful anchor.

Anchor

So to sum it all up: with zero preparation, beyond simply choosing what state you want to anchor, all you have to do is wait for that awesome moment when you close a really big sale (or any situation that causes you to organically pop into a state of *absolute* certainty, or absolute *anything*, for that matter), and then, *right then, in that very instant, when that moment hits*, you whip out your tube of BoomBoom, unscrew the cap, take a deep, prodigious blast up each nostril so you can literally *feel* the rush of the mint and citrus bathing your olfactory nerves, giving you that pleasant, invigorating burn. Then ball your hands into a pair of fists and start squeezing tightly, with your fingernails digging into your palms so you can really feel it, and belt out the word "yes" in a forceful yet controlled manner, so the bulk of the volume and power is directed inward, right to your solar plexus, where it resonates with your heart and soul and liver and loins and your very gizzard itself. And that's it.

You've just set yourself an extremely powerful anchor that you can use the next time you're about to enter a sales encounter.

Here's how it looks, laid out in steps:

Step #1: Choose a state

Like before, let's choose a state of *absolute certainty*.

Step #2: Set your anchor

You wait for a *very specific moment*, and then take out your Boom-Boom, unscrew the top, and follow the steps above—take a massive blast up each nostril and then ball your hands up into fists and dig your fingernails into your palms, and belt out the word "yes" in a powerful yet controlled manner.

Then, ten seconds later, with the scent of BoomBoom still lingering but the initial rush gone, repeat the process again.

And that, as they say, is that.

You've anchored in a state of absolute certainty.

Now, just to be safe, you can repeat this process one more time—the next time you close the same type of awesome sale—and stack a second anchor right on top of the first one. It certainly can't hurt, as anchors become stronger when they're stacked; but, either way, even if you only set the anchor once, it should be very powerful the first time you fire it off, which should be right before you're about to enter a sales encounter. And just to make sure your anchor stays firmly locked in, for the next month or so, whenever you close one of those especially awesome sales, the ones that cause you to pop into a peak state of absolute certainty, take another one-and-one of your BoomBoom, and keep stacking anchor on top of anchor on top of anchor, until the linkage is *so* engrained that it will stay with you forever.

So that's olfactory anchoring in a nutshell.

I've seen it work its magic with countless people, who've been impacted by this in a far more profound way than I. After all, state management was always something that came easy to me in a sales or business setting; but I'm the exception to the rule. For every guy like me, there are a million others who are the exact opposite, and they are held back massively for no other reason than that they lack the ability to show up to a sales encounter being their best self.

To that end, I can't even begin to tell you how gratifying it's been to be able to throw those people a lifeline, in the form of a little black tube with a wickedly pungent smell. All it takes is a quick shot up the left nostril and a quick shot up the right, and managing your state becomes as simple as taking a few drops of Visine to get the red out.

In fact, between the awesome power of the Straight Line System and the assurance olfactory anchoring gives you that you'll be in a state that allows you to tap *into* that power, you've set yourself up to accomplish virtually anything you put your mind to.

So now let's shift back to the actual *skills* of the Straight Line System—picking up right where we left off, with a deep dive into the ten core influencing tonalities and body language principles.

7

ADVANCED TONALITY

LET'S PICK UP RIGHT WHERE WE LEFT OFF IN CHAPTER 4. START-
ing with a detailed explanation of each of the ten core tonalities that
drive human influence.

However, before I dive in, I first need to give you a quick ethical
warning regarding the *extremely* powerful unconscious communication
strategy for which these ten tonalities serve as the primary building
blocks.

When I say, "extremely powerful," what I mean is that once you become even reasonably proficient with this strategy, you can actually get
people to buy things they shouldn't buy, and do things they shouldn't
do, *without* them even realizing that an extraordinary amount of influence was brought to bear.

Now, *obviously*, a strategy like that has the potential to be seriously
abused by an unscrupulous salesperson, so I want to make sure that
it's crystal clear to every last reader that I don't condone that sort of
behavior in even the slightest way—hence, I would greatly appreciate
you signing the following ethical warning:

> *I will never use the strategy I'm about to learn to manipulate*
> *my prospects into acting against their own self-interest. If I*

do, then I deserve the same ten years of pain and suffering that Jordan had to endure.

X_____

Your Name

Remember, maintaining your ethics and integrity is the gift that every man and woman gives to themselves. Whether it's a lack of sleepless nights, being a role model to your kids, enjoying a sense of well-being, or building an impeccable reputation that creates even greater success, I can tell you from my own personal experience that there's no better feeling than achieving wealth and success without cutting any corners.

So, that being said, let's dive in.

What I've been leading up to here is the existence of an immensely powerful strategy that uses the ten core influencing tonalities to enhance your outgoing communication in a way that's *so* profound that your prospect's conscious mind finds itself struggling to keep up with all the additional words it's hearing as a result of the constant shifts in tonality.

In a matter of seconds, virtually all of its processing power is now dedicated to this one specific task—trying to keep up with the avalanche of additional words it keeps hearing—and you've taken control of your prospect's own inner monologue and have it narrating *for* you, versus *against* you.

Are you slightly confused? If you are, you're not alone.

You see, while this strategy is very easy to learn, it's somewhat harder to understand. So let me break it down for you step by step—starting with a quick refresher from the previous chapter regarding my mother's strategic use of tonality when she called my name.

If she said *"Jordan!"* in a stern, no-nonsense tone, then the additional words I heard were: "Get over here right now! What have you done!" And, conversely, if she said *"Jor-dan!"* in a singsong tone, then the additional words I heard were: "Where are you, my love? Come out, come out wherever you are!"

Now, this is just one basic example of how each individual tonality creates its own set of unspoken words that the listener hears in their conscious mind, and to which the listener then applies the appropriate meaning.

To that end, when you're speaking to a prospect in a situation of influence, their brain is actually listening to two distinct things at once: first, they're listening to the words you say and analyzing the meaning of each one, both *individually* and in the context of the overall sentence; and second, they're listening to their own inner monologue, as it debates the pros and cons of the last few words you said, based on the meaning they applied to them.

For example, let's say you cold-call a prospect named John Smith, and he picks up the phone and says hello, to which you reply, "Hi, my name is Bill Peterson, calling from the Acme Travel Company. I'm looking for Mr. John Smith. Is he home?"

Now, unless John Smith has been living under a rock for the last thirty years, there's a 99.9 percent chance that he will strongly suspect that Bill Peterson is a salesman. Precisely what product he's selling and where he got John's number from John still doesn't know, but that doesn't change the fact that this person is a complete stranger, as opposed to someone John knows.

After all, a friend, or even a casual acquaintance, would never address him in such a formal manner, and such a person would likely also have recognized his voice over the phone. And when he combines that with the fact that virtually every time his phone rings, it turns out to be a telemarketer, John knows the deal within the first five seconds of the sales encounter.

So how does he respond?

Well, in many cases, your typical "John Smith" simply hangs up the phone, confident in the fact that he won't be offending anyone he knows.

However, let's say *this* particular "John Smith" has impeccable manners and doesn't feel comfortable hanging up on someone, even if that someone is a *pushy* salesman, who's had the audacity to cold-call him in the sanctuary of his home.

So, instead of hanging up, Mr. Smith says, in a slightly annoyed tone: "This is Mr. Smith. Can I help you?"—while his inner monologue says to his critical judgment center, in a thoroughly pissed off tone: "*Shit*, another damn salesman calling my house and interrupting my dinner! I gotta figure out a way to end this call, and then I'm going to put myself on the Do Not Call List."

Now, obviously, this is not the sort of inner monologue that sets the stage for the salesman to have any reasonable chance of ultimately closing this deal. In fact, the reality is that the sale was over before it ever started. However, since all Bill Peterson heard was Mr. Smith's outward response—which was, "Can I help you?"—he is completely in the dark to this, and he continues on confidently with the sale.

"Good evening," he says. "I'm calling to let you know about an incredible opportunity in the . . . ," and as the salesman drones on, explaining this incredible opportunity of his, Mr. Smith's dialog is already on the attack.

"Incredible my ass!" says Mr. Smith's inner monologue to Mr. Smith's critical judgment center, in his prefrontal cortex. "This guy is so full of shit! If he was in front of me right now, I swear to God

I'd ring his damn neck and—" Suddenly, Mr. Smith realizes that he's being asked a question.

". . . simple as that, Mr. Smith. I just need to ask you a couple of quick questions, so I don't waste your time. Sound good?"

"Sorry, you caught me at a bad time," Mr. Smith replies quickly. "I gotta go."

"No problem," Bill Peterson replies. "What's a bet—"

Click!

And, *just like that*, the sale is over before it even started, another in a long list of "blown sales" that could have gone the exact opposite way, if the million *Bill Petersons of the world* were aware of what was happening with their prospect's inner monologue and had been taught a simple, yet immensely powerful, strategy to counter it.

Ten Core Influencing Tonalities

Before I teach you the specifics of this strategy, there's one crucial distinction that I need to go through first. It has to do with how born closers automatically apply the proper tonality to the words they say, as opposed to everyone else.

You see, when you're a born salesperson, you don't have to consciously decide which of the ten core influencing tonalities you need to apply to your words in order to take control of your prospect's inner monologue and stop it from narrating against you. Your unconscious mind provides this service *for* you automatically, and gets it right every single time.

As if by *magic*, if at any point during the sale it behooves you to sound *absolutely certain* or *utterly sincere*, or *caring and sympathetic* or *perfectly reasonable*, or any of the ten core tonalities that drive human influence, then that very tonality will get layered on top of your words, without you having to even think about it. It simply just happens.

On the flip side, though, when you're *not* a born salesperson, a literally *ginormous* group that includes over 99 percent of the population, then a breakdown in your internal communication occurs. Specifically, your conscious and unconscious minds fail to link up in a way that allows for the unimpeded exchange of information between the two.

In consequence, your outgoing communication ends up becoming a watered-down version of what you'd originally intended—lacking the richness and vibrancy that you *thought* you had expressed through the use of tonality and body language.

You see, unbeknownst to you, the tonality that you *thought* you had applied had somehow been blocked or impeded from completing its journey out of your mouth, to accompany your words, which, for their part, faced no blockage or impediment at all.

In other words, the absence of tonality—or, far more frequently, the presence of only a *trace amount* of tonality in your outgoing communication—was not a conscious choice you made; rather, you were a victim of a subpar internal communication platform that made you "tone deaf," as the phrase goes.

At the very instant that your words were escaping your lips and you heard them with your own ears, you were tricked by your unconscious mind into thinking that you sounded perfect, which is to say, that you sounded just the way you had intended to sound.

Yet, in reality, attributes like certainty, confidence, passion, enthusiasm, urgency, empathy, clarity, and other subjective qualities that characterize a well-told story or well-explained concept got *lost in translation*—victims of a one-two punch at the formidable hands of nature and nurture, which sent you into adulthood with an internal communication platform that waters down your outgoing messages by allowing your words to flow freely, while it impedes the tonality you've applied.

Now, insofar as how this impacts your ability to close, on the most basic level—meaning, when you use tonality in the traditional sense, as opposed to taking control of your prospect's inner monologue—you can draw a straight line back to the emotional component of the Three Tens to see the carnage. You see, in the absence of the right tonality, your ability to move your prospect emotionally is severely limited and your ability to close is also limited accordingly.

Remember, it's your *words* that move a prospect logically, and it's your tonality that moves your prospect emotionally. And, in addition to that, we can also use tonality at a much higher level to take control of our prospect's inner monologue and stop it from narrating against us. In fact, it's time to get specific about that.

Let's go back to the example of the well-mannered Mr. Smith and his telemarketing nemesis, Bill Peterson, from the Acme Travel Company. The only difference is that, this time, Bill Peterson is going to be armed with the tactics and strategies of the Straight Line System—starting with the simplest of all rules, which states that a salesperson should never address their prospect in an overly formal manner; instead, the salesperson should address the prospect in the way they would respect-fully address a friend.

So, instead of saying, "Hi, my name is Bill Peterson, from the Acme Travel Company. I'm looking for Mr. John Smith. Is he home?"—which is the equivalent of *death*—the salesperson should simply say, in a very upbeat tone: "Hi, is John there?"

Now, when I say, "a very upbeat tone," I'm referring to one of the ten core influencing tonalities, called the *"I care"* or *"I really want to know"* tonality. By applying this sort of upbeat, enthusiastic tonality, while virtually all other salespeople are saying the same words in a perfunctory manner, not only do I immediately stand out from the rest of the pack, but I also begin the process of taking control of my prospect's inner dialog.

In essence, this is about being fully engaged and showing great interest in speaking to your prospect. In other cases—like when you say "how are you"—it goes a long way toward establishing instant rapport with someone and establishing yourself as a person who cares and really wants to know *how* they're doing.

This tonality creates an unconscious psychological connection, because we naturally feel closer to people who express a sincere caring for our well-being.

Now, in this particular case, the additional words Mr. Smith heard after "Hi, is John there?" were: *"I really want to know!* I'm not like the rest of the salesmen who ask you that, just to get it out of the way. *I genuinely* want to speak to him!"

Now, to be clear, there *is* a sweet spot here, insofar as just how much peppiness and upbeatness you can layer onto your words until you start to sound disingenuous. In other words, you don't want to say it like Tony the Tiger says, *"It's grrrrrreat!"* I mean, you'd sound like a complete idiot if you did that. You want to be upbeat enough to get your point across, but not so over the top that you sound ridiculous.

Remember, tonality is the secret weapon of influence, because it's an unspoken language. Your prospect *hears* words without you having to say them, and gets influenced without even knowing.

So how does Mr. Smith respond?

At the same time he's hearing the additional words from Bill

Peterson's amped-up greeting and trying to process their meaning, he says, "Yeah, this is John," to which Bill Peterson immediately breaks out his second core influencing tonality, which is called *phrasing a declarative as a question*, and he applies it in the following words:

"Hi, my name is Bill Peterson, calling from Acme Travel Company in Beverly Hills, California. How are you today?"

Now, notice how each one of those three thoughts is a declaration:

1 **Hi, my name is Bill Peterson,**

2 **calling from Acme Travel Company**

3 **in Beverly Hills, California**

Now, clearly each of those three thoughts is a declarative statement, not a question. However, by phrasing them as questions, you've tapped into the power of three separate human desires simultaneously:

1 **To not be perceived as being out of the loop**

2 **To remember people we've met before**

3 **To appear generally agreeable**

Now watch what happens to the punctuation when Bill Peterson phrases those declaratives as questions:

"Hi, my name is Bill Peterson? Calling from Acme Travel Company? In Beverly Hills, California? How are you today?"

By phrasing each of these three statements as questions, back to back, you infer what's called a *microagreement*, and the additional words Mr. Smith hears are: "Right? Right? You've heard of us, right?"

Here's another example, from my personal life:

My daughter was the best salesperson when she was little. She'd say, "Daddy, we're going to the toy store, right? You said so, right?" If you've ever heard kids do that—you know that they naturally know how to use this tonality. Now, when my daughter would do this, naturally I'd go into my head and start searching my memory, thinking, "I don't know. Did I?" But she'd already moved the conversation forward and was headed out the door to go to the toy store before I could stop and really think about it. Using this tonality before I knew what was happening, she'd Straight-Lined me into the car, to the store, and into buying her the toy she wanted.

This is a tonality you want to use sparingly, but it's incredibly powerful in gaining agreement with your prospect. You can either phrase your statement as a question or, in some contexts, just use the exact words as you raise your voice again, again, and again, to which your prospect will hear: "Right? Right? Right?"

When Bill phrases his name as a question, Mr. Smith's inner monologue starts saying, "Wait a second! Am I supposed to know who this person is? I better hedge my bets and sound like I do!"

What happens in that very instant, when you phrase a regular statement as a question, is that it sends your prospect's brain into search mode, as the prospect tries to figure out whether or not they should know the person who's calling. And again, due to the conscious mind's limited processing power, as long as your prospect remains in search mode, their internal monologue is paralyzed from working against you.

Now, to be clear, as powerful as this concept is, you shouldn't delude yourself into thinking that just because you phrased a declarative as a question, your prospect is now going to buy from you. That's simply not how tonality works. Rather, it keeps the prospect in the game—by stopping their inner monologue from narrating against you—thereby, opening up the possibility for further influence by you, which will come in the form of your next sentence.

In fact, at this point in the sale, that's precisely how I want you to be thinking about things: word by word and sentence by sentence.

I want you to make sure that *each* word you've chosen is the absolute *best* one possible given your desired outcome (more on this later in the chapter on scripting), and that the tonality you've applied allows you to maintain control of your prospect's inner monologue and, as a result, the sales encounter.

In this particular instance, the next group of words you're going to say—aka, your next *language pattern*, in Straight Line parlance—is going to explain the precise reason why you called the prospect today.

In other words, you didn't just call the prospect out of the blue. You didn't call yesterday, you didn't call tomorrow, and you didn't call next week; you called right now, and there's a very specific reason for it.

We call this reason a *justifier*, inasmuch as it creates a justification for your reaching out to the prospect. I'll go through this in more detail in Chapter 10 (which goes into detail on *prospecting*), but for now all you need to understand is that when you use a justifier correctly, it will dramatically increase the compliance rate for whatever request you're making. In this case, the request that Bill Peterson is going to make will be for permission to ask Mr. Smith a series questions, so he can begin the intelligence-gathering process. However, for now, let's just focus on the justifier itself and the tonality that Bill is going to apply to it—namely, the tonality of **mystery and intrigue**.

Bill says, "Now, John, the *reason* for the call today is that we've been reaching out to a select group of homeowners in your area to offer them . . . ," and then he'll go on to explain whatever that offer happens to be. It could be a marketing special, where Mr. Smith is going to get free airfare or a free night in a hotel; or it could be the chance to join a vacation club or travel club, or anything else that offers a perceived benefit to Mr. Smith.

The way you create mystery and intrigue with this tonality is by lowering your voice to just above a whisper and then hanging on the R in the word "reason" for an extra fraction of a second.*

In addition, because you lower your voice to *just* above a whisper, the reason takes on the properties of a secret, creating a sense of urgency and scarcity, which takes us now to our fourth core influencing tonality, namely: *scarcity*.

In sales, we use the word "scarcity" to describe a prospect's natural inclination to want more and more of what he or she perceives there to be less and less of. In other words, when a person finds out that something they desire is in short supply—or scarce—it makes them desire that something even more.

All told, there are actually three types of scarcity.

The first type is called *verbal scarcity*.

Verbal scarcity is a state of scarcity created strictly by the use of words. Let's switch examples now (and say goodbye to Mr. Smith and Bill Peterson), and let's assume that you're a BMW salesman and a prospect walks into your dealership looking to buy a black 750iL with black leather interior. And say you wanted to create verbal scarcity about the model and color of car that prospect wanted.

You could say something like "We only have one black-on-black 750iL left on the floor, and it's going to be three months until our next shipment comes in." Pretty straightforward, right?

In essence, by explaining to the prospect that the car he wants is in short supply, the salesperson increases the likelihood that the prospect will buy the car now, to avoid the possibility of missing out.

In sales, we refer to this process as creating urgency, and it's an integral part of persuading your customer to buy now, as opposed to

---

* Go to www.jordanbelfort.com/tonality to hear exactly how it sounds.

sometime in the future. In consequence, you should always try to create at least some degree of urgency right before you ask for the order, as it will dramatically increase the likelihood of your prospect saying yes.

Now, if the salesperson wanted to increase that likelihood even further, then they could layer the tonality for scarcity on top of the words said.

We call this second type of scarcity *tonal scarcity*.

Specifically, tonal scarcity is when you lower your voice to just above a whisper and then put a little *oomph* into it! Applying that tone of voice to a word or phrase triggers a sense of scarcity in the listener's unconscious mind, which then sends a signal to its conscious counterpart, in the form of a gut feeling. In other words, tonal scarcity stacks on top of verbal scarcity, so that the *sound* of your words intensifies the feelings of scarcity in the prospect's gut to a level far beyond what they would have felt from words alone.

And that takes us to the *third* type of scarcity, which is called *informational scarcity*—meaning, the information *itself* is in short supply. In other words, not only is the black 750iL in short supply but also nobody else is aware of that fact.

In essence, informational scarcity compounds the effect of the whisper, turning what is said into a full-blown secret that the prospect feels they can use to gain a personal advantage.

Here's how you put it all together:

- First, *verbal scarcity* is used to convey the logic: "We only have one black-on-black 750iL left, and once it's gone, it's going to be three months until our next shipment comes in."

- Second, you add on *tonal scarcity* by using a power whisper, which greatly intensifies the prospect's sense of scarcity.

■ And third, you add on *informational scarcity* by explaining that even the information itself is in short supply.

For the next three tonalities, let's jump ahead to the end of the main body of your sales presentation, right to the point where you're going to ask for the order for the first time.

In this case, we're going to apply a series of three tonal shifts as we ask for the order—starting with a tonality of *absolute certainty*, then transitioning into a tonality of *utter sincerity*, and then transitioning again to *the reasonable man* tone.*

Let me first explain each tonality separately.

1 *Absolute certainty:* I've already explained this to you in detail in Chapter 4, so let me just quickly refresh your memory. In essence, with the tonality of absolute certainty, your voice takes a firmer, more definitive tone, with a power that seems to come right from your solar plexus, in order to convey your absolute conviction about whatever you happen to currently be saying.

2 *Utter sincerity:* This is a calm, smooth, confident, low-pressure tone that implies that what you're currently saying to the prospect is coming directly from your heart, and that you're being absolutely sincere with them at the highest possible level. It's a velvety smooth tone that's so humble, and so nonthreatening, that it sounds almost apologetic in nature, but, of course, there's no apology being given. Rather, you're telling someone something that is clearly in their best interest, and

---

* Go to www.jordanbelfort.com/tonality to hear the tonalities in action.

hence they would be a fool not to believe what you're saying and take your advice.

3 *The reasonable man:* This is one of my favorite tonalities, as it's used at some of the most important moments in the sales encounter. In this particular case, we're focusing on how it's used at the close; however, what I want you to understand is that we are also going to be using it at the beginning of the sale, when you ask your prospect for permission to explain the benefits of whatever product or idea you're offering them. In other words, you don't just start pitching your prospect an idea, without first saying something along the lines of "If you have sixty seconds, I'd like to share an idea with you. *You got a minute?*"

Those last three words—"got a minute?"—are when you apply the reasonable man tone, which entails you raising your voice up at the end of the sentence,* to imply the reasonableness of your statement.

In essence, when you use the reasonable man tone, the extra words your prospect hears are "I'm reasonable, you're reasonable, and this is a very reasonable request!" And since it's basic human nature to want to obey the golden rule—do unto others as you'd have them do unto you—your prospect feels an unconscious obligation to return your reasonableness in kind, causing them to say yes to your request.

Now, when it comes to the close, here's an example of how we put all three tonalities together into one tonal pattern.*

First, the typical language pattern for a close would be something along the lines of "If you give me one shot, Bill, believe me, you're going to be very, very impressed. Sound fair enough?"

---

* Go to www.jordanbelfort.com/tonality to listen to the tonality.

Now, let me show you how we take the above three tonalities and turn them into a very powerful tonal pattern.*

First, we start with the tone of absolute certainty, which is applied to the words "You give me just one shot, Bill, and believe me . . ."

Next, we smoothly transition from the tonality of absolute certainty to the tonality of utter sincerity, which is applied to the words ". . . you're going to be very, very impressed . . ."

And then lastly, we transition from the tonality of utter sincerity to the tonality of the reasonable man, which is applied to the words ". . . sound fair enough?" And this implies that you're a reasonable man making a reasonable statement.

Remember, you don't want to say "SOUND FAIR ENOUGH?" in an angry, aggressive tone, or "Sound fair enough?" in a nasally Poindexter tone, or "Sound fair enough?" in a high-pitched Mary Poppins tone. Rather, what you need to get across is that you're reasonable, and hence the whole thing is reasonable and it's no big deal to buy. That's how you want to finish the close, not in a tone of absolute certainty, which implies pressure.

Now, let's say you gave a great presentation, which ended with you asking for the order for the first time, but, for whatever reason—meaning, your prospect hits you with one of the common objections—they still want to think about it.

The first question you're going to ask them, no matter what objection they hit you with, is: "Does the idea make sense to you? Do you like the idea?"

That's the beginning of a language pattern that will allow you to transition into your first looping pattern, which we'll discuss later,

---

* Go to www.jordanbelfort.com/tonality to listen to the tonality.

where you're going to begin the process of increasing their level of certainty for each of the Three Tens.

So let's say in response to you asking for the order, your prospect says, "It sounds good. Let me think about it."

Your reply would be: "I hear what you're saying, but let me ask you a question. Does the idea make sense to you? Do you like the idea?"*

Now, the key here is that the tone you use—starting with "I hear what you're saying . . ." and going all the way to the end, when you say, ". . . do you like the idea?"—is going to be your *hypothetical, money-aside* tone.* The additional words that your prospect hears in this case are "Hypothetically speaking, putting money aside, does the idea make sense to you? Do you like the idea?"

In essence, you've made the whole thing an academic exercise, which totally disarms them—allowing you to continue the process of increasing their level of certainty for the Three Tens, through the process of looping.

Next, we have the tonality of *implied obviousness.**

In essence, this is an advanced form of future pacing, because you're creating the impression in the prospect's mind that the benefits of what you're selling are a *given*. If you're in finance, for example, you might say, "Now, John, *you'll make money with this*, but more importantly, what I can do for you over the long term in the way of new issues and arbitrage plays . . ."

In other words, you're using tonality to infer the notion that it's beyond obvious that your product or service is a winner.

This brings us the to last of the ten core influencing tonalities: *"I feel your pain"**—which I also refer to, on occasion, as the Bill Clinton tonality, due to his complete and utter mastery of it.*

---

* Go to www.jordanbelfort.com/tonality to listen to the tonality.

In essence, this is a tonality that you want to use when you're asking questions that are designed to uncover your prospect's primary and secondary pain points and, if necessary, amplify them.

You see, if you try to do that while using an *aggressive* or *unsympathetic* tonality, then you will instantly break rapport with the prospect, and there's an excellent possibility that they will end up despising you. However, if you use the "I care" tonality, they'll end up falling into an even deeper state of rapport with you, because they will get this powerful gut feeling that you understand them, and that you truly care.

The key to this tonality is that you're expressing empathy and sympathy, and that you truly feel their pain and deeply care about helping them resolve it. You're not just there to make a commission.

And, with that, let's move on to body language.

8

ADVANCED BODY LANGUAGE

HAVE YOU EVER MET SOMEONE WHOM YOU FOUND TRULY repulsive? Someone who, by their mere presence, made you feel so uncomfortable and so off-kilter that if you had still been in grade school, you'd have asked your desk partner to give you a cootie shot?

For all you non–East Coasters, a cootie shot is a make-believe injection given to you by a friend, to protect you from catching another kid's cooties. Common symptoms of cooties include wearing flood pants, picking your nose and eating it, a love of fossils, being chosen last for sports teams, making discombobulated arm movements while speaking, and a general grossness that announces itself from at least fifty yards away. (As an aside, it's strongly recommended that children who don't suffer from cooties treat those who do with the utmost compassion, because there's a 99 percent chance that they'll end up working for one of them when they're older.)

Whatever the case, I'm sure that, at some point in your life, you've all crossed paths with someone who triggered that type of visceral negative response in you. What I'd like you to do right now is think back to that very moment when you first laid eyes on that person and that gut-wrenching feeling first washed over you. You're almost certain to find that it was not the person's words or tonality that gave you the heebie-jeebies; rather, it was their *body language*. There was something about the way they looked or acted or moved their body or shook your hand or failed to make eye contact or stood too close to you that set off the alarm bell that rocked you to your core.

The bottom line is that nonverbal communication is ten times more powerful than verbal communication, and it hits you with the force of a cannonball to the gut. Things like thoughts and feelings and intentions are all communicated in the way that you move your body: by your management of space and time, your posture, appearance, gestures, the way you make facial expressions and eye contact, even the way you smell.

All of that gets processed in a microsecond when you are speaking to someone in person and they lay eyes on you for the first time. It's not so much that effective body language will close the deal for you. What I'm saying is ineffective body language will blow the deal for you. It stops you or doesn't allow you to get into a rapport with someone else; they are repelled by what they see.

When a person lays eyes on you for the first time, in that 1/24th of a second that their judgment indicator goes up and down, they see your face and how you move and they make a judgment. In essence, they rip you apart, process you in their brain, then put you back together and you are judged.

Either you are being judged as a person who is sharp, on the ball, someone they want to do business with, or you're being judged as someone they do not want to do business with, which is to say: someone who repels them, someone who they perceive to not be an expert or to not be sharp or enthusiastic. All those things that you need to get in tight rapport.

Here's a story to illustrate how repulsive negative body language can be. It happened at a seminar I gave in Sydney, Australia, one of my favorite cities in the world. I had just gone through the whole section on body language in detail, delved into all the particulars of eye contact, how you shake hands, how close you stand to somebody.

I was on that last issue of how close you stand for fifteen minutes, calling people on stage and allowing them to experience for themselves how awful it feels when someone invades your space bubble. So everyone is getting it, everyone is right in tune.

I take a short break, and as soon as I walk off the stage, some wacky Australian comes running up to me, with his thick accent, saying, "Yo, mate, mate, mate!" He gets right in my face, and I'm thinking, "Oh my god." The guy continues to invade my space, all the while saying, "I got this thing, I got this thing, mate, mate, mate." As I am tuning out and covering my face to stop the spit that's being rained down on me, this guy is trying to explain his revolutionary invention called the Express Loo.

Express Loo? Turns out it's a porta-potty for five-year-olds, and he wants to demonstrate, right then and there, how you use this little wooden thing. Anyway, long story short, he ends up corralling not just me but my Australian manager, my seminar promoter, and everyone else in earshot. In every case, he runs up to the person and gets right in their face. And every person walks away with the same exact feeling, which is: "I don't know about his product, but I would never do business with this guy in a million years."

The bottom line is this: body language is not going to get you the sale, but the wrong body language will destroy the opportunity to make a sale.

The things a person will internally debate start with a very basic observation: your appearance. They'll then make a snap decision about you as a result of that. It's like we discussed in item number one on the syntax. They'll be debating things like how clean-cut you are, if you're well dressed or not, how much jewelry you're wearing. It all goes back to judging a book by its cover. How someone dresses, how long their hair is, how they groom themselves, how they shake hands—it all makes a huge difference in how we're perceived and, for that matter, how we perceive other people.

For instance, when a man wears a suit and tie, we immediately perceive him as someone who has his shit together: a *person of power*, so to speak. Same thing goes for a woman, although we're talking about a power suit in that case. A pantsuit or a skirt is fine, but the skirt should be no higher than just above the knee, and there should be no excessive makeup, jewelry, or perfume. Too much of these things can undermine a woman's credibility.

Remember, *sex sells*—for both men and women—but only in a Dolce & Gabbana ad or a Calvin Klein commercial, not in the work-place. If a man or woman wants to be taken seriously, they can't come to work dressed like they're going to a nightclub, or coming from the gym. It sends the wrong signal and undermines their credibility. But this whole idea of *wrapping your package*, as the phrase goes, extends far beyond clothing and perfume. It cuts through to everything.

Let's start with men's facial hair.

Anything more than a closely cropped beard or mustache, and you should shave it. It gives off an untrustworthy vibe. It also hints at a lack of pride and a lack of attention to detail. Now, there are a few exceptions to this, of course, like if you're selling Harley-Davidsons for a living, or if you're in a part of the world, like the Middle East, where a beard is customary. But, generally speaking, unkempt facial hair is a definite no-no.

The equivalent of an unruly beard for a woman would be an ex-treme hairdo of some kind. It's just the sheer *excess* of it all. It makes you wonder, "What's wrong with this person?" The same thing goes for excessive jewelry. It's a major negative, both for a man *and* for a woman, albeit for entirely different reasons.

Can you guess what's the worst thing a man can wear, in terms of creating a perception of mistrust?

A pinky ring, especially if it has a big, fat diamond on it. There's nothing more toxic than a diamond pinky ring when it comes to inspiring mistrust. It gives off the distinct whiff of you being a sharpie— someone who's on the *make*. A hustler, but one who's dressed in an expensive suit . . . and who wears a pinky ring.

That being said, there *are* certain circumstances where a pinky ring is actually appropriate, such as if you're the host at a casino, or if you work behind the counter of a jewelry store. It's called the *Law of Congruency*, and it fits into the same category as my Harley-Davidson example. In other words, the best way to dress is in a style that's congruent with your profession.

A plumber, for instance, shouldn't be wearing a suit and tie when he shows up at your door to give an estimate. Not only would it look ridiculous, but you might also take it as a sign that he's going to overcharge you because he needs to pay for more suits!

Conversely, if the plumber showed up at your door looking like a total slob, then you'd probably be concerned that his work would be as sloppy as he is. And nobody wants sloppy work done on their plumbing. Based on the Law of Congruency, he should wear a crisp, clean uniform with his company logo on the front and his name embroidered onto the shirt. He should be holding a clipboard, and on it should be a blank estimate form, ready to be filled out.

A male insurance agent should be in a suit and tie. He should wear little if any cologne. If he wears too much, he'll be perceived as a sharpie. A female insurance agent should be in a power suit, with just enough makeup and jewelry to show that she takes pride in her appearance but isn't defined by it. And she should be carrying a leather briefcase, but not a Hermès one or one made from crocodile. If she likes perfume, then just a hint.

This is all actually pretty easy to get once you understand the principles behind it. Think back to all of the salespeople you've met over the years who violated these rules—all the stockbrokers and insurance brokers and real estate agents and car salesmen . . . doesn't it amaze you that they were ignoring these easily fixable errors?

The funny thing is, at the time, you couldn't figure out exactly why you didn't trust those people, or why you didn't feel like they had your best interest at heart. But now you know, and it all seems pretty obvious in retrospect. Tools like these help you get into an unconscious rapport very quickly.

But let's not jump ahead. For now, remember that getting into a rapport with someone is done primarily through tonality and body language, not your words. In terms of body language, I've talked about *wrapping your package*, but there's so much more. For instance, males and females respond very differently to certain types of body language, and the rules, of course, change accordingly.

Let's start with spatial awareness. If you're a man selling to another man, then you want to do what's called *cornering off*—meaning you want to stand at a slight angle to another man, as opposed to directly in front of him. When a man faces another man, it creates for many a feeling of conflict and hostility, and it instantly takes the men out of rapport. So what you do to avoid this is you *corner off* with the other man—meaning you shift your body position so you're at a slight angle to him, which has the effect of immediately disarming him.

If you're a man, try it yourself sometime. You'll be shocked at how much more natural it feels than standing face-to-face with another man. It's almost like letting air out of a balloon when you corner off. You feel an immediate release of pressure.

For communication with a woman, though, it's the exact opposite. If you're a man trying to influence a woman, the woman wants you to stand directly in front of her and keep your hands above waist level, where she can see them.

Conversely, if you're a female trying to influence another female, then you definitely want to corner off, just like a man with another man; however, if you're trying to influence a male, then you definitely want to stand directly in front of him. Either way, what you don't want to be is one of those dreaded *space invaders*—those people who invade another's space bubble. (They are usually *spitters* too!) In the Western world, the space bubble is about two and a half to three feet. You want to maintain at least that much distance between yourself and your prospect when you're standing next to them. Otherwise, you run the risk of being branded a space invader. *Space-invading spitters* make you want to take out an umbrella and use it as a spit guard.

However, there *is* one exception to the space invader rule, and that's in Asia. People tend to stand a bit closer in Asia, marking about a *half-foot* difference.

The Asian culture, like all unique cultures, has its own norms. As such, in general, Asians pay particular attention to body language, especially when it comes to establishing status. Take their formal bow, for instance. Who bows lower, and who rises first, instantly establishes the power hierarchy of the parties. For the Asian culture, bowing is the cornerstone of a successful greeting, similar to the way the handshake is to Americans. On that note, the way you shake hands says a lot more about you than you actually think. It can set you up to quickly get into a rapport with someone, or it can eliminate that possibility entirely.

Have you ever had someone grab your hand and shake it like you were a rag doll? What were you thinking while you were coming out of your shoes and your hair was flopping around? Was it something along the lines of "What the hell is wrong with this person?"

When someone starts shaking your hand like that, they might *think* they're making a good first impression, but they're actually not. In fact, all it does is make you wonder what they are trying to prove. *Are they looking to establish power over me? Are they trying to intimidate me?* The same thing goes for the opposite type of handshake—the so-called *dead fish* approach. This is where they extend their limp hand, which hangs like a piece of overcooked spaghetti, and just hold it there, like they don't really give a shit. We hate it because it's actually the ultimate power handshake. It's like someone's saying to you, "I don't care what the hell you think about me. I'm so far above you that you're not even worthy of me shaking hands with you in an appropriate manner."

The best handshake for getting into a rapport with someone is called the *cooperator's handshake*, which is your basic, neutral handshake, where you meet someone's hand head-on. You're not above them or below them; you're even with them, and you return the same pressure they give to you. It's part of an overall rapport-building strategy called *matching*, which has to do with entering a prospect's world and being where they are. (More on this later.) However, in this context, *matching* means that if someone shakes your hand firmly, then you should shake theirs just as firmly—up to a *point*. I mean, you don't want to get into a squeeze-off with somebody, where they shake your hand really hard, so you try to shake theirs even harder, to which they shake yours even harder, and then you try to outdo them again. You don't want to be like, "Okay, big shot! I'll show you!" You're better off letting them *out-squeeze* you a bit, while you maintain good, solid eye contact, so they know they haven't intimidated you.

Speaking of eye contact, here's an interesting fact: if you don't make eye contact at least 72 percent of the time, people won't trust you. There have been detailed studies on this stuff, and 72 percent is the number. You can look it up online. Anything more, and you risk getting into a stare-off with somebody.

The magic number is 72 percent. It's enough to show that you care and that you're engaged in the conversation, but it's not *too* much. Basically, it's not so much that you look like you have something to prove.

One more thing about body language: watch the position of your arms. Someone who crosses their arms can be communicating that they are closed to new ideas. Arm positioning is one of the most basic elements of body language—being open versus being closed—and it's obviously very easy to spot.

Now, just because someone's arms are crossed doesn't mean that they're definitely closed to new ideas. They might just be cold, for all you know. Of course, if I had a choice, I'd want my prospect's arms in an open position versus closed. All things being equal, it *does* usually mean that someone's more open to your ideas. But I definitely wouldn't take it as the ultimate sign.

When you pay attention to body language, you'll notice something fascinating. If I'm sitting in front of you with my arms crossed, and then uncross them, you will likely do the exact same thing—without even realizing it. It's not some kind of Jedi mind trick. It's called *pacing and leading*. It's the next level up from *matching*, which is what I spoke about before when we were talking about handshakes. With *pacing and leading*, you're basically kicking it up a notch, by *pacing* them, *pacing* them, and then *leading* them in the direction that you want them to go.

When it's done right, it's an immensely powerful strategy, and it works with both tonality *and* body language.

Active Listening and the Art of Matching

Before we dive more deeply into pacing and matching, let's discuss another important concept: *active listening*. This is a way of listening to someone that helps you actually build rapport with them. One of the greatest misconceptions about tonality and body language is that they only come into play while you're the one doing the talking. In fact, how you move your body, the facial expressions you make, how you smile, and all those little grunts and groans you make as someone's talking to you—those are all part of the technique I call *active listening*, and it's a powerful way to get into a rapport with someone.

Let's start with something as simple as nodding your head while your prospect is speaking. When you nod your head, it shows that you get what that person is saying; that you're on the same page. The same thing goes for facial expressions, like when your prospect starts talking about something that's very important to them. You want to look straight into their eyes, with your own eyes narrowed a bit, and with your mouth crooked to the side. Then you add an occasional nod, along with a few *ahas!* and *yups!* and *I got its!*

Now, if that was my body language while you were explaining your problems to me, what would you think about me? Would you think that I was really listening to you? That I truly cared?

Yes.

There are other facial expressions too—like compressing your lips and lowering your head a bit, which implies sadness, or compressing your lips and nodding your head slowly, which implies sympathy and empathy. The master of this type of body language is President Bill Clinton. Back in his prime, he was the absolute *best*. He'd shake at least a hundred hands a day, and he had only a split second to earn someone's trust, and he could do it every time. It seemed that from the second when he shook your hand and you fell into his magnetic zone, you got the feeling that he really cared about you. That he felt your pain.

As for the audible cues, the *ahas!* and *yups!*, they're more effective at *maintaining* rapport than actually building it. They let the prospect know that you're still on the same page with them; that you get what they are saying. The audible cues are even more important when you're on the phone and don't have body language to rely on. In that case, those little grunts and groans are the only way to stay in rapport with your prospect while they're talking.

When you're in person, though, you can also use *matching*—essentially adopting the same physiology as your prospect to slide into rapport with them. Some examples of this are the position of their body, their posture, and also their breathing rate. Even how fast they blink can be matched.

Matching is an incredibly powerful tool for getting into a rapport with someone, especially when you're in person and you can match both body language *and* tonality. But it can also be extremely effective over the phone too, if you focus on matching not just someone's tonality, but also their rate of speech and the type of words they use, including any slang.

And before you think I'm saying something creepy about copying someone, let's review again. You're not copying, you're *matching* them; there's a big difference. Copying someone is called *mirroring*, meaning that you actually try to mirror your prospect's physical actions in real time, as they're doing them. If they scratch their nose, then you scratch your nose, and if they cross their legs and lean back in their seat, then you cross your legs and lean back in *your* seat. Now, that *is* creepy, and it's also obvious, which is something I'm not a fan of at all.

But I *am* a fan of matching, which means that if your prospect leans back in their seat, then you lean back in your seat too, but you do it slowly, casually, after a five- or ten-second lag. In the end, it all goes back to *likability*—meaning that people want to do business with people who are basically like them—not *different.* You start that process by entering a prospect's world where they are, which sets you up to slide into rapport. Then you want to *pace* them, *pace* them, and then *lead* them in the direction that you want them to go. This is a really powerful tool when you use it right.

Remember, there's pace, pace, lead . . . and then there's *Pace! Pace! Freaking Lead!* That's the way *I* teach it: ninja-style, on steroids. What I mean by this is that they don't see it coming. Don't forget that pacing is one of those things in life that needs to be done exactly right, or else it won't work. But when you actually *do* get it right, then *watch out!* Not only will it help get you into a super-tight rapport with someone, it will also help you change his or her emotional state from a negative one to a positive one and increase the level of certainty.

One story I like to tell about this is the time my son, Carter, came home from soccer practice absolutely furious about this kid on his team who was a major ball hog. That night, my fiancée said, "Carter is really, really upset. Why don't you go downstairs and see if you can calm him down?"

Here's what I *didn't* do: I didn't walk downstairs, acting all soft and sympathetic, like I was trying to calm him down. I didn't drop my tone and say, "Listen, buddy, I know you're really upset right now, but you shouldn't let someone get to you like that. It's not good for you."

Why? Because then he'd have gotten even *madder*. He'd have been like, "Don't get upset? What do you mean don't get upset? The kid's a damn ball hog! I hate him! *Everyone* hates him! He should be thrown off the team!" And then I'd say, "Whoa, whoa, whoa! Calm down, buddy. It's no big deal. Relax for a second." At which point he'd get even *madder*. He'd be like, "*Bullshit!* It *is* a big deal! I'm *not* gonna calm down!"

By trying to enter his world in a calm state, when he's in an aggravated one, I'd only have aggravated him more. So, instead, I matched him. I walked in acting as pissed off and angry as he was. In fact, I acted even angrier. I said, my voice booming, "What the hell is going on, Carter? I know that bastard of a kid is a ball hog! We've got to do something about it right now! Should we call the coach and get him thrown off the team?"

Then he matched me, just like I knew he would. He became just as angry as he thought *I* was, and he said, "Yeah, let's call the coach! Let's get him thrown off the team! That kid's a menace!" To which I said, "Yeah, let's do that, buddy!" And, just like that, I began lowering my voice and taking on a more sympathetic tone. Then I shook my head sadly and said, "I don't know, buddy. I wonder what causes him to act that way. You think he has some emotional problems?" And then I softened my voice even more, and added, "It really is a shame."

And, of course, Carter started shaking his head sadly too. He said, in tones as sympathetic as mine, "Yeah, it really is, Dad. I guess I should feel bad for him. He's probably really unhappy."

And just like that, he calmed down.

Matching can be a way to calm *anyone* down, or get them excited about something, or feeling certain about something. You simply enter their world where they are, and then you *pace* them, you *pace* them . . . and then you *lead* them in the direction you want them to go.

Now, I didn't invent pacing and leading. It's been around since the very dawn of human communication. All great communicators do this. They do it naturally, without even thinking about it. But *anyone* can learn it, once they know the rules.

Remember, the next step in the system, which is the simultaneous gathering of intelligence and building rapport, is more about what your prospect will say to you than what you'll say to your prospect. In fact, the best way to explain this to you is to go through a simple, yet very powerful, exercise.

The time has now come for me to sell you a pen.

9

THE ART OF PROSPECTING

"SELL ME THIS PEN!"

The first time I sprung this on a cocky young salesman, I was sitting behind my desk in my office at Stratton, and what I got in return was a very telling response.

"You see this pen?" chirped the cocky young recruit, sounding like he'd just walked off a used car lot. "This is the most amazing pen money can buy. It can write upside down, it'll never run out of ink, it feels great in your hand.

"*Here*, check it out for yourself; tell me how *great* it feels." And, with that, he leaned forward in his seat and extended his arm across my desktop and offered me the same disposable pen that I'd handed to him a moment earlier, to begin the test.

Playing along, I grabbed the pen and rolled it around in my fingers for a few seconds until it slid into its usual writing position.

"Pretty damn amazing, right?" he pressed.

"It feels like a pen," I replied flatly.

"That's exactly my point!" he exclaimed, ignoring my lukewarm response. "That's how a great pen is *supposed* to feel—like it's been a part of you for *years*.

"Anyway, it's obvious that you and this pen were made for each other, so I'll tell you what I'm gonna do: I'm gonna take *30 percent* off the regular purchase price, but"—he raised his right index finger in the air, for a moment—"only if you buy it right now. Otherwise, it has to go back up to the normal price.

"Either way, it's a really great deal, but at 30 percent off it's the deal of the century. Whaddaya say?"

"What do I *say*?" I shot back. "You mean *besides* the fact that you're obviously completely full of shit?"

No response. The would-be Strattonite just sat there completely still, with a panic-stricken look on his face.

"That wasn't a rhetorical question. You want me to ignore how completely full of shit you are, yes or no?"

He slowly opened his mouth to speak, but no words came out. He just sat there with his mouth hanging open.

"I'll take that as a yes," I continued, deciding to let the kid off the hook. "So, putting that small detail aside for the time being, I will say that I'm not in the *market* for a pen right now.

"I don't want one, I don't need one, I barely ever *use* one; and, in truth, if I ever *do* decide to go out and buy a pen, it won't be a piece of shit like this. I'd probably pick up a Mont Blanc or something.

"But how could you possibly know that?" I continued, zeroing in on the main point of the exercise. "In fact, how could you know *any-thing* about me? From the second you opened up your mouth, all you did was spew out a bunch of cheap sales talk.

"'The pen is this,'" I chirped, mocking his used car salesman rap, "'the pen is that, the pen writes upside down, it's your long lost brother'. . . and blah, blah, fucking blah. Even if you put aside how utterly ridiculous that sounds, did it ever occur to you to maybe ask me a *few* questions *before* you attempted to ram a pen down my throat? Like, am I even in the *market* for a pen? Do I have a certain price range in mind? Do I prefer one *type* of pen to another?

"I mean, think about it for a second: how could you try to sell me something without knowing the *first* thing about me? It completely defies logic."

The would-be Strattonite nodded his head sheepishly. "So, what should I have said?"

"You tell me," I shot back.

Just then the door swung open and Danny walked into the office, wearing a $2,000 suit and a cynical expression. "You almost done with this?" he asked.

"Almost," I replied, "but I'm actually glad you popped in. Your timing is perfect. I need you to do something for me."

"What's that?" he answers cautiously.

"I want you to sell me this pen!" I declared, grabbing another pen off my desktop and extending my hand towards him.

Danny shot me a look. "You want me to sell you a pen. *Seriously?*"

"Yeah," I fired back. "Show the kid how it's done. Sell me this pen."

"Fine, I'll sell it to you," he muttered, grabbing the pen and taking a moment to examine it. Then, all at once, he completely changed his demeanor and flashed me a warm smile and said, in a respectful tone: "So, tell me, Jordan, how long have you been in the market for a pen?"

"I'm not in," I replied. "I don't use pens."

"Really? Well, then you can have your lousy pen back," he snapped, tossing the pen back onto my desktop.

Then he looked at the kid and said, "I don't sell things to people who don't need them. I leave that to novices, like you."

While the moral of the story seems plainly obvious, there's actually a lot more going on here than meets the eye. So let me take things one at a time, *starting* with the obvious:

Firstly, it should be crystal clear to you by now that trying to sell something to someone who doesn't need it or want it is a fool's errand and a total waste of time.

A Straight Line salesperson, and for that matter any *professional* salesperson, would never consider shooting from the hip like that. Instead, they would sift through their prospects as quickly and efficiently as possible, separating out the ones who were interested from the ones who weren't.

In general sales parlance, this sifting process is referred to as "qualifying a prospect," and the primary method by which a prospect gets *qualified* is by answering a series of questions that get posed to the prospect by the salesperson.

All in all, it's a cut-and-dried, no-frills process that's utilitarian in nature and gets straight to the point. If upon answering your questions, it turns out that the prospect needs what you're selling, and can afford to pay for it, then they are qualified. It's as simple as that.

And then you use the Straight Line System, where the word "qualifying" is never to be uttered under penalty of . . . well, not *death*, but, at least, *shame*.

Here, we refer to this process as "Straight Line prospecting," and the primary method by which we do our sifting is through *gathering intelligence*.

Now, if you recall, I touched on this topic at the end of Chapter 2, when I presented you with a flashback from the night when I first invented the Straight Line System.

When you gather intelligence, I explained, you want to know everything there is to know about your prospect, so long as it's relevant to closing the sale—including their needs, beliefs, values, *hierarchy* of values (meaning, the relative importance of each value), their past experiences with similar products, past experiences with other salespeople, personal financial situation (insofar as affording your product), and both their primary and their secondary pain points.

On top of that, what I *also* explained that night—and what I want to reemphasize now and dig into more *deeply*—was the fact that your ability to gather intelligence will be directly related to how powerful a first impression you made on your prospect during those first four seconds.

In other words, the only way that your prospects will answer your questions honestly and forthrightly is if they perceive you as being a *true* expert in your field, and a person whose confidence and eloquence and bottled *enthusiasm* has left them no doubt whatsoever that you're *definitely* a person worth listening to, someone who can help them achieve their goals and resolve their pain.

Without that, there's simply no reason for your prospects to waste their time opening up to you or risk the embarrassment or loss of confidentiality that could result from it. So instead, they'll only give you perfunctory answers to your questions or, more likely, they'll try to take control of the sale themselves, causing things to spiral out of control.

I've seen it happen a thousand times:

A novice salesperson tries to qualify a prospect, only to have the prospect answer their questions with questions of their own, until the whole thing has devolved into chaos. It's a perfect example of the Iron Mike Tyson metaphor I used at the end of Chapter 2. The only difference is that instead of getting barraged by devastating punches, you're getting barraged with devastating *questions*—*devastating* in the sense that they'll cause you to veer off the Straight Line and go spiraling off to Pluto or, even worse, Your-*anus*.

Conversely, when *you* are in control, the barrage *stops*. Realizing that they are in the presence of an expert in their respective field, the prospect feels compelled to defer to you, and allows you to ask as many questions as you deem necessary, *without* interruption.

Now, this latter point is absolutely *crucial,* because in the absence of interruptions, questions can now be asked in a manner and sequence that not only promotes a smooth, mutually productive intelligence-gathering session but also *enhances* your ability to build rapport. But I'm jumping ahead now.

Straight Line prospecting has more moving parts than any other step in the syntax, so the most effective way to teach it to you is to start with the big picture first.

Let me zoom out for a moment and give you a quick overview of the relationship between marketing and sales—insofar as how they work hand in hand with one another to turn a company's goods and services into cash—and how Straight Line prospecting serves as the bridge between the two.

In essence, you have *marketing* on one side of the equation, and *sales* on the other. The objective of *marketing* is to:

1 **Research the marketplace to identify the best prospective buyers—*prospects,* for short—for a particular product.**

2 **Develop a cost-effective strategy that gets the company's message in front of as many of these prospects as possible.**

3 **Embed the message with some sort of *offer* or *hook* or call to action that prompts as many of these prospects as possible to enter the company's sales funnel.**

4 **Coordinate with the sales department to ensure a seamless handoff of the funnel, so prospects can be turned into customers.**

Now, in *today's* world, there are two types of marketing.

First, we have *offline marketing*, which includes everything that takes place *off* the Internet—TV and radio ads, newspaper ads, magazine ads, billboard ads, direct mail, telemarketing, network marketing, educational marketing, door-knocking campaigns, etc. And, second, we have *online marketing*, which includes everything that takes place *on* the Internet—Google ads, Facebook ads, Twitter ads, YouTube ads, banner ads, landing pages, opt-ins, retargeting campaigns, email blasts, affiliate marketing, SEO campaigns, and much, much more.

Now, as I said, whichever marketing modality a company decides to use, the ultimate objective is always the same: to bring as many qualified buyers as possible into the company's sales funnel, so they can then be handed off to the sales department and turned into customers.

Pretty straightforward, right?

Actually, not quite.

You see, no matter how carefully you target your marketing campaign, there is no possible way that every prospect who enters your sales funnel will end up being a qualified buyer. In fact, in *most* cases, if even *half* of those prospects turn out to be qualified buyers, then you're doing great.

In essence, this is what Straight Line prospecting is all about: sifting through prospects who enter your sales funnel to eliminate the ones who don't qualify to buy your product—thereby avoiding wasting your time making a full-blown sales presentation to them.

To that end, in any given marketing campaign, there are four categories of buyers who will enter your sales funnel. We call these the four buying archetypes.

The first archetype is called *buyers in heat*.

These are basically your *best*, most motivated buyers. These prospects want your product, need your product, can benefit from your product, can afford your product, and, most importantly, they're prepared to make a buying decision *right now*.

Like all legitimate buyers, *buyers in heat* have a certain pain they're looking to resolve; however, what separates them from the rest of the pack is that they've already made the decision to *do* something about it now. In other words, they're *done* waiting; they're ready to act. They've gotten to the point where they are simply no longer willing to tolerate the pain that comes from an unresolved need, so they've decided to get proactive.

The only downside to this group of ready-made buyers is that there aren't that many of them. Depending on what industry you're in and how targeted your marketing campaign was, you'll find that somewhere between 10 and 20 percent of the total prospects that enter your sales funnel will fall into this category; the rest will be spread among the other three.

The second buying archetype is called *buyers in power*.

These are your *second* best group of buyers. The primary difference between the first two archetypes is that buyers in power aren't consciously feeling any major pain from their unfilled need, which causes them to lack the same level of urgency as buyers in heat.

In other words, while buyers in power have every intention of buying the type of product you're selling, their lack of urgency makes them feel like they're in a position of power, so they're not going to pull the trigger until they're done shopping around and have made themselves absolutely certain that they've found the best solution to their problem.

Nonetheless, these are still excellent prospects (and there are also a heck of a lot more of them than buyers in heat!). On average, somewhere between 30 and 40 percent of the total prospects that enter your sales funnel will end up falling into this category.

At the end of the day, it's the prospects from these two

categories—*buyers in heat* and *buyers in power*—who will make it past the intelligence-gathering phase and continue their journey down the Straight Line. The prospects from the remaining two buying archetypes need to be weeded out as quickly as possible, *especially* those who fall into the third archetype:

The dreaded *lookie-loos*.

Also known as "tire-kickers," the lookie-loos are the most danger-ous prospects that will enter your sales funnel. What makes them so destructive is that they disguise themselves as buyers in power—*acting* as if they're genuinely interested in buying your product—while they actually have no intention of doing so. In consequence, they continue their journey down the Straight Line, as opposed to getting weeded out during the intelligence-gathering phase as they're supposed to be.

The resulting damage occurs on two levels:

First (and most obviously), it causes a massive amount of time to be wasted as you end up making full-blown sales presentations to prospects who have no intention of buying. And second (and even more damaging) is the confusion and negativity it creates as a novice salesperson tries to figure out why their closing rate is so low. "Is there something wrong with *me*?" the salesperson wonders. Is it their pitch? Is the salesperson not making a strong enough logical case? Emotional case? Or maybe the salesperson is screwing up at the very end, during the objection-handling phase? After all, the prospects remain interested the whole way through—giving the salesperson buy signal after buy signal to the very end—and then they don't buy.

You see the problem here?

Having no idea that between 30 and 40 percent of their sales funnel is filled with professional time wasters (disguised as buyers in power), salespeople end up spending the bulk of their time making sales pre-sentations to prospects who have no intention of buying.

The good news is that identifying them isn't very difficult.

There are four telltale signs that will alert you to the fact that you're having your time wasted by a lookie-loo:

1 They tend to ask lots of questions that they seem to already know the answers to.

2 They make it a point to *kick the tires* of whatever it is you're selling, almost to the point of *over*-kicking them.

3 They let out a large number of *ooos* and *aahs* and *yups*, to reinforce the sense that they're genuinely interested.

4 When asked about their finances, they either become boisterously overconfident or unnecessarily vague.

Again, I can't overestimate the importance of being hypervigilant when it comes to identifying and weeding out the lookie-loos as quickly as possible. You'll end up avoiding a lot of pain over the long run.

Now, this takes us to the fourth and final buying archetype, which I refer to as *the mistakes*, or "the people who were dragged there." In essence, these are people who never belonged in your sales funnel in the first place. Either they clicked on the wrong website, showed up at your place of business by mistake, or they were simply *dragged* into your sales funnel by someone else.

Whatever the case, the common thread among all the *mistakes* is that they had no desire to enter your sales funnel in the first place, so you have basically no chance of closing them.

So, in summary, the three main goals of Straight Line prospecting are as follows:

1 Identify the lookie-loos and the mistakes and remove them from your sales funnel as quickly as possible.

2 Gather the necessary intelligence from the buyers in heat and the buyers in power, and then continue moving them down the Straight Line towards the close.

3 Begin the process of turning the buyers in power into buyers in heat by amplifying their pain.

Now, insofar as number 3 is concerned, there's a lot more to this concept than it makes sense to discuss now, so let me circle back to it when we get to the next chapter, which covers the ten core distinctions of Straight Line prospecting.

In fact, let's dive into that chapter right now.

It's time to take you from the theory of Straight Line prospecting to the real world application of it.

The next chapter will show you precisely how you get there.

10

THE TEN RULES
OF STRAIGHT LINE
PROSPECTING

WHEN YOU'RE PROPERLY ENGAGING IN THE PROCESS OF STRAIGHT
Line prospecting, you're doing each of the following four things:

1 You're sifting through the prospects in your sales funnel by
asking them a series of strategically prepared questions.

2 You're using these questions to not only gather intelligence
but also to separate the buyers in heat and buyers in power
from the lookie-loos and the mistakes.

3 You're continuing to gather intelligence from the buyers in
heat and buyers in power, while eliminating the lookie-loos
and mistakes from your sales funnel as quickly as possible.

4 You're transitioning the buyers in heat and the buyers in
power to the next step in the syntax, so they can continue
their journey down the Straight Line.

Insofar as the ten rules of prospecting are concerned, they are meant
to provide you with everything you'll need to create a practical blue-
print for gathering intelligence in your industry.

Now, as you go through each rule, you should keep relating it back to your own situation—making whatever changes are needed to your current method of prospecting. To that end, if you have a prospecting script or a list of intelligence-gathering questions, then you should have those in front of you before we begin.

So, grab those now, and let's get started.

Rule #1: You are a sifter, not an alchemist.

Imagine yourself as one of those old-fashioned gold prospectors, who kneels at the edge of a stream with your trusty tin pan, sifting through thousands of gallons of water, as you patiently wait for that one nugget of gold to drop into your pan.

It's a sight that we've all seen countless times, both in the movies and on TV: an old miner, with his scraggly beard, playing the waiting game by the edge of a stream. He'll wait there as long as he has to, knowing full well that sooner or later a nugget of gold will present itself.

However, what he's *not* waiting for is for the water *itself* to turn into gold. That's a job for an *alchemist*, not a prospector.

You see my point?

Water is water and gold is gold; they're different elements that don't magically convert into one another, any more than lookie-loos and mistakes convert into buyers in heat or buyers in power.

That's why a salesperson has to become an expert sifter, not an alchemist. There's simply no two ways about it.

Rule #2: Always ask for permission to ask questions.

As easy as this distinction is to execute, virtually all untrained sales-people ignore it, simply because they're unaware of how negatively it will impact their ability to get into rapport.

Plain and simple, unless you ask for permission to ask questions, you run an extremely high risk of being perceived as the Grand Inquisitor–type, instead of a trusted advisor, and the Grand Inquisitor–type does not "care about you," nor are they "just like you," which are the two driving forces behind getting into rapport.

However, the *good* news here is that all you have to do to avoid this outcome is remember always to ask for permission to ask questions. It's as simple as that.

Below are a few sample language patterns that get straight to the point and have been proven to work:

- "John, just a couple of quick questions, so I don't waste your time."

- "John, let me just ask you a couple of quick questions, so I can best serve you."

- "John, let me ask you just a couple of quick questions, so I can see exactly what your needs are."

Any one of the above examples will set you up for a non-confrontational intelligence-gathering session that promotes the building of rapport.

In addition, I want you to notice how I use the word "so" in the second half of each of the three examples. In this context, we refer to the word "so" as a justifier, because it justifies your need to ask the prospect questions, as opposed to doing it out of curiosity or nosiness.

In essence, in order to do your job correctly, there are certain things that you need to know in your capacity as an expert. By using a justifier, you can get that point across to your prospect loud and clear, and it paves the way for an even more productive intelligence-gathering session.

Rule #3: You must always use a script.

I'm only going to touch on this rule briefly, as the entire next chapter is dedicated to the creation of scripts and how they roll up into one cohesive presentation.

One of the key reasons why you want to always use a script for prospecting is that each industry has its own unique set of questions that need to be asked in a certain order.

If you try to *wing it*—as opposed to having all your questions mapped out in advance, in precisely the right order—then the chances of you remembering all the questions, or asking them all in the right order, is slim to none, and each mistake you make will have a negative impact on your ability to gather intelligence.

Another major benefit of using a prospecting script is that since you already know what words you're going to say, your conscious mind is freed up to focus on applying the right *tonality* to your words, as well as on what your prospect is communicating back to you.

Are there any clues in their facial expression, or their tone of voice, or their general body language?

Again, I'm going to be digging into this in much greater detail in the following chapter, so let's move on.

Rule #4: Go from less invasive questions to more invasive questions.

By asking non-invasive questions first, you give yourself the opportunity to start building rapport by actively listening to your prospect's answers. It's almost like peeling back the layers of an onion. Each non-invasive question that your prospect answers creates an even tighter state of rapport, which paves the way for you to ask successively more invasive questions.

Let me quickly show you how the wrong approach looks, using

a stockbroker gathering intelligence from a wealthy prospect as an example.

After a brief introduction, during which the broker took control of the sale by establishing himself as an expert, he transitioned to the intelligence-gathering phase by asking for permission to ask questions, using the *reasonable man* tonality, to which the prospect replied, "Sure, go ahead," which is how you can expect virtually every prospect to respond—provided that you've established yourself as an expert and asked for permission to ask questions using the correct tonality.

And now comes the broker's first question, which is:

"So, tell me, John: how much money are you liquid for right now—including both your personal bank accounts and your different brokerage accounts around Wall Street? *Oh*, by the way, please include any mutual funds you have as well, as long as you can liquidate them within seven days."

"Excuse me?" snaps the prospect, in a tone of incredulity. "I don't even know you. Why on earth would I answer that?"

"Oh, I'm sorry," says the broker, in an apologetic tone. "Let me start with something else. What was your annual income last year, including any capital gains?"

No response.

"Just a ballpark," the broker adds, trying to prod the prospect into answering. "You can round—"

Click!

"Hello?" says the broker to an empty telephone line. "Are you still there, John? Hello . . . *hello?*"

And, *just like that*, the sale is over before it even started.

With a huff and a puff, the prospect smashed the phone down in the broker's ear, and had every justification to do it.

After all, the broker had simply not earned the right to ask him those types of invasive questions yet. Not only did he lack the required level of trust and rapport, but he also lacked the benefit of having an intangible aspect of human communication on his side—namely, the mitigating effect of *desensitization*.

By way of definition, psychologists describe desensitization as a diminished emotional response to an adverse stimuli after repeated exposure to it. In laymen's terms, it simply means that we have a tendency to quickly get used to things.

For example, something that you would normally find wholly offensive—like being asked an invasive question by someone who you hardly know—will barely cause you to raise an eyebrow after just a few minutes of desensitization; and that's especially true when it comes to someone gathering intelligence from you, as a result of the lubricating effect that comes from suddenly finding yourself in rapport with the person asking the questions.

Again, I can't overestimate how crucial this distinction is to ensuring a successful outcome to an intelligence-gathering session.

Ignore it at your own peril.

Rule #5: Ask each question using the right tonality.

In Chapter 11, which details how to make a sales presentation, I will provide you with a list of big-picture questions that have been proven to work in any industry, along with their accompanying tonalities.

For now, what you need to understand is that each prospecting question will have its own "best" tonality, which maximizes the chance of your prospect giving you the most forthright answer, while also ensuring that you maintain rapport with them in the process. Conversely, if you apply the wrong tonality to your question, then your prospect will answer it in a perfunctory manner at best; and while you might not completely *break* rapport, you will certainly bring the level down a few notches.

Here's a quick example.

Let's say you're a life insurance salesman, and you're at the home of a prospect trying to close him on a whole life policy. Given that life insurance is a fear-based sale, it's especially crucial that your intelligence-gathering effort not only uncovers his primary pain point but also amplifies it, as this will be the key to closing the sale.

To that end, here's an example of an invasive question you might ask, to begin the process of ferreting out the source of his pain:

"So, John, all things considered, what's your biggest fear right now with not having a life insurance policy in place? What's really keeping you up at night?"

Now, imagine if you attached a callous, almost aggressive tone to those words, as if you were chastising him for being so foolish and irresponsible for not having adequate life insurance coverage in place.

It would be like you were saying to him, "So what's your greatest fear, John? Tell me! Tell me! Come on! Let's go! Tell me!"

Now, of course, you didn't actually say those extra words—*Tell me! Tell me! Come on! Let's go! Tell me!*—but that's precisely what he heard as a result of tonality's ability to add extra words onto our communications. And what he also heard was his own inner monologue saying, "This guy is a total asshole! He doesn't care about me; he doesn't feel my pain; and he's not sympathetic to my plight."

Alternatively, if you had used the "I care" tonality, along with "I feel your pain," then the extra words your prospect would have heard would have said, "Wow, this guy really cares about me; he really genuinely wants to know."

So, again, if you attach the *wrong* tonality to your question, it will cause you to break rapport with your prospect while also eating away at your credibility as an expert. Conversely, if you attach the *right* tonality to your question, it will cause an increase in the level of rapport while also reinforcing your position as an expert.

Remember, this applies to every question you ask during the intelligence-gathering phase. There are no "free" questions.

Rule #6: Use the correct body language as the prospect responds.

This too relates back to what I covered in the previous chapter, when I went through the body language principle of *active listening*—as well as distinction #4 of this chapter, where your ability to actively listen as your client answers your questions will serve as the linchpin strategy for building rapport as you move through the intelligence-gathering process, with your goal being to hit a high note as you prepare to transition into the main body of your sales presentation.

In consequence, you need to be absolutely vigilant about following all the active listening rules that I laid out for you in Chapter 8—starting on page 132. Below is an abbreviated list of the active listening techniques that you'll most frequently use during the intelligence-gathering phase:

1 Nodding your head while your prospect is speaking. This shows that you understand what they are saying and that you're on the same page as them.

2 Narrowing your eyes and compressing your lips, while nodding your head slowly, when your prospect is disclosing an issue that's very important to them.

3 Narrowing your eyes even more while compressing your lips more intensely, if the above topic deals with one of the prospect's pain points. In addition, you'll continue to nod

your head slowly while letting out the appropriate *oohs* and *aahs* to show that you actually feel your prospect's pain.

4 Leaning forward when you ask an emotionally charged question, and then continuing to lean forward while your prospect answers (while also using the active listening techniques I laid out above in number 3).

5 Leaning back when you ask a question that's grounded in logic, and continue to lean back and nod your head in understanding and scratch your chin thoughtfully while your prospect answers.

While the above list assumes that the sales encounter takes place in person, for many of you that will not always be the case. So when the encounter takes place over the phone, your active listening will be distilled down to the various *oohs* and *aahs* and *ahas* and *yups* that you let out as your prospect responds to your questions. This will let the prospect know that you're still on the same page as them, and that you *get* what they are saying.

Rule #7: Always follow a logical path.

The human brain is extraordinarily adept at analyzing a series of questions and determining whether or not they're being asked in a logical order. If they're not, then it will serve as a major red flag that the person who's asking them is not an expert in their field.

For example, imagine being on the receiving end of the following series of intelligence-gathering questions, asked in exactly this order:

1 What part of town do you live in?

2 Are you married or single?

3 What kind of work do you do?

4 How long have you been living here?

5 Do you have any children?

6 What do you like most about your neighborhood?

7 Are you self-employed or do you work for someone else?

Frankly speaking, if you'd been asked these questions in an actual sales setting, by the time you reached question number four, your internal monologue would have been raging away, a mile a minute, saying things like: "What the hell is wrong with this guy? He seemed like an expert at first, but he obviously has no idea what he's talking about. Let's get this nonsense over as quickly as possible and find a *real* expert, not an impostor like this guy."

By the way, if you think I'm exaggerating, I'm *not*.

The *good* news, though, is that this entire issue is easily avoided. All you need to do is take the time to engage in a little strategic preparation—which, in this particular case, means making a complete list of your prospecting questions, and then keep arranging them in different orders until you hit on the one that stands out as the most logical. (Trust me when I say that the right order will be plainly obvious to you. This will be easy pickin's, now that I've raised your level of awareness.)

In fact, let's do a quick practice run with this right now, using the list of seven questions beginning on the previous page. If you recall, I purposely arranged them so they'd be out of logical sequence. What I want you to do now is take out a pen and paper (or you can use your smartphone or computer) and make a list of all seven questions in their most logical sequence.

Once you've done that, you can find the correct order below.

1 **What part of town do you live in?**

2 **How long have you been living there?**

3 **What do you like most about your neighborhood?**

4 **Are you married or single?**

5 **Do you have any children?**

6 **What kind of work do you do?**

7 **Are you self-employed or do you work for someone else?**

Notice how these questions make perfect sense in this order.

In fact, not only does each question pave the way for the ones that come after it, but also each of your prospect's responses will begin to paint a picture of a certain aspect of their life that you can fill in with more and more detail by asking follow-up questions based on their responses.

Just make sure that when you ask your follow-up questions you exhaust each line of questioning before you move on to the next one. And don't ping-pong back and forth between your prepared questions and your follow-up questions, as it will break the logical flow.

Remember, at this point in the sale, it's extremely rare that any one mistake will be damaging enough to cause a one-punch knockout; rather, it will be like death from a thousand cuts.

In other words, each one of your mistakes or incongruencies—whether it's asking a question out of the logical sequence, attaching the wrong tonality to it, getting overly invasive before you've earned the right to, or forgetting to actively listen to your prospect's responses—will slowly but surely eat away at the rapport you've worked so hard to create while also undermining your position as an expert, until you reach the point where one more mistake is enough to act as the proverbial straw that breaks the camel's back.

Rule #8: Make mental notes; don't resolve their pain.

When you're qualifying a prospect, all you should be doing is asking questions and making mental notes based on their responses. You do not want to try to resolve their pain at this point. In fact, if anything, you want to amplify that pain.

Remember, pain serves as a warning signal that there's something wrong in their life—something that they need to take action to fix—so if you take them out of pain *before* you make your presentation, then you're actually doing them a huge disservice.

In other words, when a prospect reveals their pain to you, you don't want to jump the gun and say, "Oh great! There's no need to worry now! My product is going to take away all your pain, so there's no longer any reason to feel bad anymore. Just sit back and relax while I explain everything to you."

If you do that, then you're shooting yourself in the foot in a massive way. You see, by applying a temporary balm to their pain, you're transforming your prospect from being a buyer in heat to being a buyer in power, which is the exact opposite of what you want to be doing.

Instead, you want to amplify their pain by asking them a series of follow-up questions that actually *future pace* it—forcing them to experience the reality of being in even *greater* pain at some point down the road if they don't take action now to resolve it.

This will ensure that your prospect not only *understands* the ramifications of not taking action to resolve their pain, but also *feels* those ramifications in their gut.

Rule #9: Always end with a powerful transition.

The purpose of a transition is to move those prospects who are going to continue their journey down the Straight Line to the next step in the sales process, which is when you make your Straight Line sales presentation.

In addition, this is also where you're going to eliminate the lookie-loos and the mistakes, as well as any buyers in heat and buyers in power who aren't quite right for your product.

You see, the simple fact is that not every buyer in power and buyer in heat should be taken farther down the Straight Line. For example, if your product is not a good fit for them, then you have a moral obligation to tell them that—to explain that you can't help them, and that they really shouldn't be buying.

You should say something along the lines of:

"Well, John, based on everything you just told me, this program isn't a particularly good fit for you. I'm really sorry about that, but I don't want to sell you something that you're not going to be thrilled with." And if you happen to know of another company that *can* help them, then you should direct them there. Of course, you're not morally obligated to do this, but it's definitely the right thing to do.

Remember, today's unqualified prospect can be tomorrow's perfectly qualified prospect, and the amount of goodwill you establish by sending them somewhere else is incalculable. In fact, I've had situations where I did just that, and before I could even leave the table, the prospect started calling their friends to try to drum up business for me; and I've also had situations where a year later I got a call out of the blue from someone I did that for, and now that person was ready to buy.

Now let's talk about the other side of the equation—where after gathering all the necessary intelligence, you're 100 percent certain that your product can resolve your prospect's pain and improve the quality of their life.

In that case, you would use a simple transition like this:

"Well, John, based on everything you just said to me, this program is *definitely* a perfect fit for you. Let me tell you why . . ." Or you could substitute the word "product" for "program"—or use the actual name of either one.

In that case, it would sound like this:

"Well, John, based on everything you just said to me, the *64-inch Samsung* is *definitely* the perfect fit for you. Let me tell you why . . ." And from there, you'll go directly into the main body of your sales presentation.

Rule #10: Stay on the Straight Line; don't go spiraling off to Pluto.

In 2009, I was hired by a London-based seminar provider to do a private sales training for the company's twenty young salesmen, who were struggling so badly that they could barely close a door.

When I was maybe halfway through the first day of training, I passed by one of the salesmen's desks and heard him going off on some crazy tangent about duck hunting in the marshes of southern England.

As it turned out, the subject of duck hunting had been raised by his prospect in response to a standard intelligence-gathering question that the salesman had asked him a few minutes earlier, a standard question that had absolutely *nothing* to do with shooting a bunch of innocent ducks. (The question he'd asked was: "What kind of work are you currently doing?")

And, to be clear, the prospect didn't start his response by talking about duck hunting; rather, he answered the question that he was asked—telling the salesman that he was mid-level manager at a clothing manufacturer in Kent—but then rather than leaving it at that, the prospect decided to spiral off to Pluto by segueing into a long, drawn-out story about how the duck hunting in the Kent marshes was the best in all of England.

In truth, these sorts of compound answers, where the prospect starts by answering your question and then finishes by spiraling off to Pluto, are very common during the intelligence-gathering phase and are in no way problematic.

What *is* problematic, however, is the disingenuous way in which the salesman handled it.

"Oh my god!" he exclaimed, as if he were completely bowled over. "What a coincidence this is! I love duck hunting too! What are the odds—I mean—for you and me to both love duck hunting? I can't even begin to tell you how much . . ." And on and on the salesman went, going back and forth with his prospect for fifteen minutes—*fifteen minutes!*—spewing out a bunch of nonsense about the exhilaration one gets from taking potshots at a bunch of innocent ducks who can't shoot back.

Now, don't get me wrong: I'm not against duck hunting any more than I'm for it, although I *would* like to think that if you're going to take the life of an unsuspecting duck, you'd at least have the common courtesy to then baste the little guy in orange sauce and make him into a gourmet meal. Either way, what's far more important is that you understand just how misguided this salesman's strategy was. Let me explain what I mean.

A moment after the salesman slammed his phone down in defeat, he turned to me and muttered, "Damn it! I was so close. I can't believe I let that one slip away."

"No, you weren't close," I replied flatly. "You never had a shot. You were too busy talking about duck hunting. I assume you made all that shit up, right? I mean, you don't exactly strike me as the duck hunting type. Where are you from, India?"

"Sri Lanka," he replied meekly, looking down at the floor to avoid making eye contact.

"Sri Lanka. Not exactly the world's duck hunting capital, now is it?" I said with a chuckle. "Anyway, why did you lie to the guy like that? What did you think you were going to accomplish?"

"I was trying to build rapport," he said defensively, "like you said this morning."

"Wow, lesson learned!" I said to myself. "That's the last time I stress how important something is without also explaining how to actually do it."

"Fair enough," I said to the salesman. "This one's on me. But, for the record, what you just did is the exact opposite of what I meant."

Ten minutes later, I had the entire sales force back in the training room, and I was standing before my trusty whiteboard, filling in the blanks from my morning training session.

"Let me tell you a little something about rapport," I said confidently. "It is by *far* the single most misunderstood word in the English language. In fact, what most people think constitutes rapport is actually *repulsive*—meaning, it repels people instead of attracting them, which is the exact opposite of what you're trying to accomplish with rapport in the first place.

"Now, after listening to a bunch of your sales pitches this morning, it's obvious that you guys think that if you pretend to like whatever your prospect likes, you'll end up getting into rapport with him." I paused for a moment to let my words hang in the air. Then I plowed on.

"Bullshit!" I sputtered. "There's no rapport there! People are far more skeptical than they used to be, and they're constantly on the lookout for that sort of bullshit. And make no mistake, if your prospect has even the slightest inkling that you're trying to pull something like that, then

any chance you had of closing the sale completely evaporates. Make sense to everyone?"

All twenty salesmen nodded their heads in unison.

"Excellent. Now, in addition to that, what you're also doing is sending a subliminal message to your prospect that you're not really an expert. You see, experts are far too busy to waste time talking about things that aren't germane to the prospect's outcome. Their services are in demand, and an expert's time is his most valuable commodity.

"Also, experts are qualifying a prospect; they ask their questions in a very specific way—one that's both logical *and* intuitive—and they don't go off on tangents. That's what a *novice* does; they tend to be all over the place, and they're constantly going off to Pluto.

"Now, again, genuine rapport is based on two things.

"First, that *you care*—meaning, that you're not just looking to make a commission; you want to help your prospect fill his needs and resolve his pain. Basically, you have his best interest at heart, as opposed to your own.

"And, second, that you're *just like him*—meaning that human beings want to associate with people who are just like them, versus the exact opposite of them. Let me give you a quick example.

"You wouldn't go check out a country club to see if you want to join, and then come home to your wife and say, 'Guess what, honey? I went to this really cool country club today! There wasn't a single soul there who was anything like me. They all had different politics, different religions, different interests; all in all, I didn't have a single thing in common with any of them! So I joined.'

"Now, if you did that, your wife would look at you like you were out of your mind. However, your decision would have made perfect sense to her if you'd said, 'I went to this really cool club today. The people there were just like us. They all shared our politics, our religious beliefs, our family values, and almost all of them play tennis. So I joined!'

"The bottom line is this: We don't associate with other people based on our differences; we associate based on our commonalities.

"However, that being said, this is precisely where you guys are all making the classic mistake. You see, the way you think that you're supposed to accomplish this is by playing the *pretend* game—like, if he loves fishing, then you love fishing; and if he loves duck hunting, then you love duck hunting; and if he loves going on safaris, then you love going on safaris, and on and on.

"Now, I'll get into the ethical ramifications of this later, insofar as how totally unacceptable it is for you guys to be lying through your teeth like that, but for now, let me repeat what I just said to you guys about the efficacy of doing this—specifically, that it's a complete bunch of bullshit! There's no rapport there; that's actually repulsive to people.

"In fact, I'll give you a real world example, using something I heard one of you guys rambling about this morning . . ." And with that, I spent the next minutes giving the group a comical account of the duck hunting fiasco I'd been subjected to that morning, in order to keep the mood light.

When I got to the point in the story where the prospect had just spiraled off to Pluto, I began mercilessly poking fun at the salesman for his decision to join his prospect there—spending over fifteen minutes orbiting that barren rock as the two of them went back and forth about the *frickin'* wonders of duck hunting!

Then, changing to a more serious tone, I added, "But still, in his defense, it wasn't like he could just cut his prospect off in mid-sentence when he started spewing out all that duck hunting nonsense. And, by the way, guys, I'm just using his call as an example; the same thing applies to all of you.

"When your prospect starts to spiral off to Pluto, you're not going to say, 'Whoa, whoa, whoa! Now, listen, pal, I'm an expert in my field, and, as an expert, I don't have time to listen to your worthless drivel about the price of tea in China. So I want you to stop rambling about this nonsense and answer my questions directly, so we stay on the Straight Line.'

"If you do that, it's not going to go over very well with your prospect, now will it! In fact, in that scenario, you'll end up destroying whatever rapport you've built up, and you might as well end the conversation there.

"Instead, what you want to do in that situation is actually let your prospect spiral off to Pluto while you *really* step up your active listening, so he knows that you understand *exactly* what he's talking about and that you find it exciting and interesting. Of course, you're not going to actually say those words; but your tonality and body language will be more than enough to carry the day.

"Then, after he's finally done orbiting Pluto, all you need to say is something along the lines of 'Wow, that's totally cool. It sounds really interesting. I can see why you feel that way. Now as far as your goal for learning how to trade currencies goes . . .' And then you lead him back to the Straight Line and pick up right where you left off by asking him the next question on your list. *That's* how you maintain control of the sale and build massive rapport at the same time. Make sense, everyone? Raise you hands and say 'yes' if it does."

The entire sales force raised their hands on cue and let out a collective "Yes."

"Okay, great," I continued. "The *key* here is that you always remember that rapport is not a constant; it goes up and down throughout the sale, depending on the following two things:

"One, how your prospect thinks and feels about the last point you made; and two, his belief as to whether or not you are on the same page with him, in regards to that point.

"To that end, if he feels *positively* about the last thing you said, then the level of rapport *increases*; and if he feels *negatively* about it, then the level of rapport *decreases*. Likewise, if he believes that you are on the same page with him, then the level of rapport *increases*; and if he believes that you are not on the same page with him, then the level of rapport *decreases*.

"Now, guys, the reason that this is so *absolutely* crucial is because you can't close a sale while you're out of rapport with your prospect; it's that simple.

"So, if at any moment you sense that you're falling *out* of rapport with your prospect, then you need to stop, regroup, and make a conscious effort to get *back into* rapport, using the active listening protocol I laid out for you, along with two specific tonalities I went through this morning—'I care (I really want to know)' and 'I feel your pain.'

"In essence, guys, building rapport is an ongoing process. It's not like you get into rapport with someone and you can say to yourself: 'Okay, check! Now that I've got *that* out of the way, I can start acting like an asshole again!' That's not going to go over very well.

"The simple fact is that you need to be *actively* building rapport throughout the entire sale, 100 percent of the time, without ever letting your guard down. Any questions?"

"Are you going to talk about scripts?" asked one of the salesmen.

"Indeed I am," I replied. "Right now."

11

THE ART AND SCIENCE OF MAKING WORLD-CLASS SALES PRESENTATIONS

WHILE REVEALING THE SECRET TO *CHARISMA* MIGHT SEEM AN odd way to begin a chapter on sales presentations, if you give me the benefit of the doubt for the next few pages, you'll quickly see that it's not.

Let me explain why.

Firstly, when we speak of charisma, as it relates to sales, we're talking about that special charm or appeal that certain salespeople seem to possess that allows them to effortlessly slide into rapport with their prospects. It's an attractive force that's almost *magnetic* in nature, and its impact can be felt in a matter of seconds.

A perfect example of this would be President Bill Clinton, who back in his heyday was not only one of the greatest salesmen in political history but also a Jedi master in the art of charisma. Whether you loved him or hated him, to see him on the campaign trail was like attending a master class in charisma's practical application.

Moving from town to town, he would shake hands with over a thousand voters a day, having only an instant to connect with each of them; yet, somehow, when it was finally your turn—and he locked eyes with you and offered you that sympathetic smile and a few choice words—you got an overwhelming sense that not only did he *care* about you but that he also *understood* you and felt your pain.

At the end of the day, it's these three distinctions—*he cares about me, he understands me,* and *he feels my pain*—that serve as the very foundation on which all rapport is built, and they come naturally to those who possess massive charisma.

In fact, the power of charisma is so vital to a salesperson's success that it's almost impossible to find even a single top producer who doesn't possess it in massive quantities. Working like motor oil in a car engine, it lubricates each step of the sales process while setting the stage for a healthy collaboration based on trust and respect and *esprit de corps.*

But what about all the people who *don't* possess an abundance of charisma? What are *they* supposed to do? Are they *screwed,* as the phrase goes—meaning, charisma is an inborn personality trait that each of us possesses at a fixed level—or is charisma a learnable skill that can be mastered through practice?

Thankfully, the answer is the latter.

In fact, not only is charisma an entirely learnable skill but it also possesses that highly coveted Good Enough Factor—meaning, all you have to do is become *reasonably* proficient and you'll start seeing the benefits straightaway.

Now, insofar as just how you go about doing that, I've tested a number of different strategies over the years, and I've found that the quickest way to teach this to someone is to break charisma down into its three core components and teach them one at a time.

So, let's do that right now, starting with charisma's first component, which is *the effective use of tonality*—meaning, that you sound *so* good when you speak that you keep people hanging on your every word as opposed to them tuning out, or dividing their attention among other people in the room.

The second component of charisma is the targeted use of *body language*—meaning, you're being hypervigilant about applying all ten body language principles, with a heavy emphasis on active listening, to communicate an extraordinary level of attentiveness and empathy.

And charisma's *third* component—which is typically the toughest one of all, for most people—is *not saying stupid shit.*

In fact, I've seen the same scenario unfold a thousand times:

A salesperson is saying intelligent things for the first four or five minutes of the encounter and is in complete control of the sale. Then, things start to drag on a bit, and the salesperson begins running out of intelligent things to say and suddenly—*bam!*—the stupid shit starts flowing out of their mouth like it just bubbled up from out of the Brooklyn sewer system.

Even worse, once it starts flowing, it keeps getting stupider and stupider with each passing moment, until it reaches a point of such undeniable stupidity that an alarm goes off inside the prospect's mind, flashing—*"NOVICE ALERT! NOVICE ALERT!"*—at which point any chance of closing the sale is gone.

After all, if there's one thing all your prospects will have in common it's that they all know what experts should look like and sound like, and they also know what they don't look and sound like.

Experts (*mostly*) say smart shit; they (occasionally) say bullshit, and, at times, they even shoot the shit, but the one thing they *don't* say is stupid shit. *That* esteemed honor is reserved for novices, or, more accurately, for those who *sound* like novices.

You see, in the world of sales, there's a massive difference between *being* an expert and sounding like one, and, for better or worse, it's the latter that gets you paid. To that end, one of the true beauties of the Straight Line System is that it allows any salesperson, whether they're a stone-cold rookie or a world-class expert, to deliver a flawless sales presentation on a consistent basis, no matter how long the encounter drags on; and the way the system accomplishes that can be summed up in one word: *scripts*.

That's right—*scripts*.

But not just *any* scripts; I'm talking about Straight Line scripts—or, more accurately, a *series* of Straight Line scripts that work together as a cohesive unit and run the entire length of the sales presentation.

So, what is a Straight Line script?

In short, a Straight Line script is the well-thought-out essence of the perfect sale. In other words, imagine taking the ten best sales presentations that you've ever made for a particular product and going through each one of them line by line, with an eye on choosing the best passages from each and then combining them into one, ultra-perfect presentation that will become your template for all sales encounters going forward. That's what I mean by a Straight Line script.

It's basically all of your best sales lines, arranged in exactly the right order—starting with those all-important first four seconds and continuing on straight through to the end, at which point your prospect will either buy, or you will end the sales encounter in a respectful way.

In other words, if the prospect chooses *not* to buy, then you're not going to berate them or put undue pressure on them or slam the phone down in their ear or walk around muttering curses under your breath. Instead, you're going to end the call in an amicable, respectful way by saying something along the lines of: "Thanks for your time, Mr. Smith. Have a nice day."

Now, in terms of the literally *countless* benefits created by a well-written Straight Line script, I could spend two or three chapters writing about that alone; let's go through the most important benefits first, with a focus on how they work in conjunction with the rest of the Straight Line System to get you to the point where you can close anyone who's closable.

1   I know this is an obvious one, but I had to include the crucial benefit of the sale being able to drag on for as long as necessary, without there being the *slightest* risk that a salesperson will start saying stupid shit.

2   You can figure out what tonalities you're going to apply beforehand, which ensures that not only will you sound totally awesome but you'll be able to take control of your prospect's inner monologue and stop it from narrating against you.

3   You can now be sure that, no matter how nervous you are or how much of a novice you might be, when you open your mouth to speak, the *best* possible words are going to come out every single time.

4   Since your conscious mind no longer has to worry about coming up with the proper words to say, you can now focus the bulk of your attention on how your prospect is reacting to what you say. This will significantly enhance your ability to gauge where your prospect currently is on the certainty scale, as well as alert you to any slip in rapport—as a result of something that you said to your prospect that they disagreed with, or that rubbed them the wrong way.

5   It allows you to build the perfect airtight logical case for each of the Three Tens, while ensuring that you follow every Straight Line presentation rule, which, collectively, have been proven to maximize prospect engagement and increase your closing rate (I'll be going through those shortly).

6 It allows a company's management to systemize its sales force by ensuring that the salespeople are saying exactly the same thing to their prospects, regardless of what region they're in and whether they're selling inside the office or out in the field. This type of *uniformity* is absolutely crucial when it comes to growing and expanding a company's sales force, and it's the responsibility of the company's sales manager to enforce this.

7 It reduces regulatory problems by preventing a salesperson from exaggerating or making outright false statements. You see, more often than not, a salesperson doesn't purposely lie to a prospect or try to deceive them; the salesperson simply runs out of intelligent things to say, at which point they start saying stupid shit. The problem is that there are actually two varieties of stupid shit: the first variety consists of stupid shit that's truthful and accurate, and the second variety consists of stupid shit that is not truthful or accurate, which is to say it's against the laws of God and man, the latter of which can be extremely unforgiving, if you're in a regulated industry.

Again, these are just a few of the many, many benefits that are automatically enjoyed by any salesperson who uses a Straight Line script that follows the eight basic rules for constructing them.

But, still, in spite of that, and in spite of the countless challenges that consistently pop up when any salesperson, other than a natural-born closer, enters a sales encounter without having the benefit of knowing *what* they are going to say before they have to say it, there is still an inordinately large number of salespeople who have a major negative anchor toward the use of scripts.

Ranging in severity from a mild bout of nausea to a full-blown case of anaphylactic shock, their negative responses are based on three concerns: first, they think that using a script will make them sound wooden and inauthentic (or *scripted*, as the phrase goes); second, they think that their prospects will figure out that they're reading from a script and consider it *disingenuous* or the telltale sign of a novice; and third, they think that using a script is unethical or it lacks *integrity*, because of the contrived nature of a script.

On the surface, some of those arguments do seem to make a bit of sense. I mean, if someone were to hand me a script that was written in a way that would make me sound *wooden* or inauthentic, then I'd be the first one to toss it in the garbage or, better yet, light the thing on fire and then stomp on it a few times for good measure.

In fact, I did that very thing, eight years ago, in the offices of a financial services firm that had hired me to teach their sales force the Straight Line System. At the time, they employed twenty salesmen whose performance was *so* dismal that the CEO referred to them as the Bad News Bears of the financial services industry.

At the heart of the problem was a horrific telemarketing script that had been written by the company's sales manager, a thirty-something dilettante whose *own* sales ability seemed to begin and end with the line of bullshit he'd been able sell the CEO regarding his ability to manage a sales force.

In any event, the script was about three times the size of a standard piece of letter paper, and virtually every inch of it was covered in writing. The words had been *chunked* into short paragraphs, about thirty of them in all, and the paragraphs were arranged in a series of concentric circles that were connected by arrows of varying lengths and thicknesses.

Within ten seconds, I was 100 percent certain this particular script was the biggest piece of shit I'd ever had the displeasure of laying my eyes on. (And that's saying a lot when you consider how awful the average non–Straight Line script is.)

Anyway, right before we broke for lunch, I called the entire sales force into the training room, including the sales manager, and without any warning or lead-in, I held up the offending item and said, in a tone laced with venom:

"You see this script? This is the biggest piece of shit I've ever read through in my entire life! In fact, it's *so* bad that it's been sucking the life out of you guys, like a killer zombie." I shrugged my shoulders. "That's why it needs to be permanently destroyed, with no chance of resurrection. Anyone here know how to permanently kill a zombie?"

"With fire," declared a salesman. "You gotta burn it!"

"Exactly," I replied. "That's why I brought this." And I reached into a shopping bag that was sitting on the floor beside me and pulled out a handheld blowtorch that was normally used for firing up a cigar, and I held it up for public inspection.

"There will be no resurrection!" I sputtered, and without saying another word, I held the blowtorch to the edge of the script and pressed the ignition button and set the script ablaze.

With great pride, I declared, "A script needs to be a perfect straight line, not a circular piece of smeg—"

I was cut off in mid-sentence by the sight of the flame being unnaturally squelched out. Apparently, the paper had been treated with some kind of fire-resistant coating. "Can you believe this shit?" I muttered. "This script is *so* cold that it won't even catch fire!" With that, I threw the script on the floor and began jumping up and down on it, as the entire room clapped and cheered in approval—or, should I say, the entire room sans the sales manager.

Sensing his impending doom, he had slipped out of the training session while I was trying to torch his script, and he was never seen or heard from again. But nobody cared—*least* of all the company's CEO, who watched in awe as his sales soared by more than 700 percent the following month. It was a truly shocking result, he remarked in a handwritten thank-you note I received from him shortly thereafter. In addition to the note, there was also a hefty bonus check inside the envelope, with a yellow Post-it attached to it. It said:

J,

    You deserve every penny of this! Just make sure Ol' Mel gets his cut, too!

The "Ol' Mel" he was referring to was none other than Mel Gibson, of *Braveheart* fame; and the specific context he was referring to was a metaphor I had used to explain the relationship between an expertly written Straight Line script and mastering the art of reading that script without *sounding* like you were reading it.

"Now, I assume you guys have all seen the movie *Braveheart*," I said to his sales force. "Well, you know that scene where the ragtag Scottish army is standing there dressed in their torn-up kilts, holding their pitchforks and axes, and across the field is the massive army of English redcoats, who are standing in perfect formation with their archers and heavy horses and the infantry, who are all holding longswords, and it's obvious that the Scots are about to get their asses kicked. You guys all know the scene I'm talking about, right?"

They all nodded their heads.

"Great. And then Mel Gibson comes riding up on his horse, with his face all painted blue, and he breaks into that famous speech, where he says, 'Sons of Scotland, you stand here today in the face of three hundred years of oppression and tyranny and blah-blah-blah' . . . and he goes on and on, with all this incredibly motivating stuff—talking about how their entire lives have come down to this one moment, and how they have only one shot at freedom; and, *just like that*, they go charging full steam ahead at the English army and they wipe them out in a matter of minutes.

"It's an incredible scene," I said confidently. "But let me ask you one important question: You think Ol' Mel winged it?

"In other words, do you think Mel, as the director, said, 'Okay, what we're going to do here is line up a couple of thousand extras in that open field over there, and then I'm gonna set up all the cameras in just the right places, and wait for the sun to be at *just* the right angle, and then right when I give them the cue to flee, I just ride out there on my horse and motivate the hell out of them and convince them to stay, so they can kick some serious redcoat ass!'

"Now, if any director were to actually do that, just imagine what would come out of Mel Gibson's mouth when he galloped onto the field, especially if he had a couple of drinks in him!

"But, of course, no director would ever do something so reckless. With only one shot for a character to say exactly the right thing, they ensure their success by hiring an expert screenwriter to come up with the perfect lines for the character to say, and then they hire a world-class actor (Mel didn't have to look far when casting himself), who will not only memorize his lines but also use perfect tonality and body language to bring the scene to life."

So, what's the moral of the story?

Well, there's actually more than one, but the point I was trying to drive home was that if you're part of that group of salespeople who think that, by their very nature, scripts are going to cause you to sound wooden or inauthentic—making it extremely difficult to get into rapport with your prospects and move them emotionally—then you need to consider one very simple fact, which is:

Since the time that you were old enough to talk, every single movie or TV show that made you laugh or cry or scream or shout, or that got you so deeply invested in the characters that you ended up binge-watching the entire series in a single weekend; every last one of them was *scripted*.

In fact, even the reality shows you watch—which use the authenticity that *supposedly* comes from being an *unscripted* show as a powerful tool to drive viewership—are all scripted!

You see, it didn't take long for the producers of these shows to realize that when they didn't hand the *reality stars* a script of some kind, and they let them wing it instead, the end product was so awful and tedious that the show became unwatchable.

So if you want to hang on to the false belief that using a script is going to make you sound wooden and inauthentic, because sounding wooden and inauthentic is an inherent characteristic of using a script, then you need to ignore the fact that you've spent about half of your life being made to laugh and cry and scream and shout as a result of—yes, you got it: scripts!

The key to success here is actually twofold: first, you need to become proficient in the art of reading from a script without sounding like you're reading from a script; and second, you need to become proficient in the art of writing a script that will allow you to sound perfectly natural when you read it.

In Straight Line parlance, we refer to this process as *strategic preparation*. It's an attitude that borders on overpreparation. In short, the philosophy of strategic preparation is based on anticipating everything that might possibly come up in a sale and having the best possible response to it prepared in advance.

In fact, that's what the rest of this chapter is all about: the construction and delivery of a Straight Line script.

So let's start by going through the eight things that set Straight Line scripts apart from everything else out there. In essence, these are the key features that must be in place in order for your script to be effective.

First, your script must not be front-loaded.

Front-loading is when you disclose all your major benefits right up front, which leaves you with nothing powerful to say to change your prospect's mind when they hit you with the first objection.

This is one of the biggest mistakes salespeople make: they think they have to mention every single benefit when they make their initial sales presentation. In consequence, they end up with a script that's a mile long, and the prospect is zoned out before they're even halfway through. The key to writing a great script is to frame, not front-load.

It's like framing out a new house: you have to do it in stages. First you put up the actual frame, then the drywall, then the paint. It's the same thing with a sale. You can't expect to close so soon. There are going to be objections, so be prepared for a prolonged battle. You have to get your foundation in place first.

In essence, human beings are not built in a way where we go from zero to 100 mph in one shot. There have to be these little stopping-off points, where we can take a deep breath and consolidate our thoughts. In other words, the way you raise someone's level of certainty is bit by bit; you can't do it all at once.

Second, focus on the benefits, not the features.

While there's no denying that this is Sales 101, for some inexplicable reason, the average salesperson tends to gravitate towards focusing on a product's features, not its benefits.

Now, to be clear, I'm not saying that you should never mention a product's features; if you didn't, you would sound totally ridiculous, as you'd just be talking about benefit after benefit after benefit, without providing your prospect with any context for what actually created the benefit. The point is that you want to briefly mention a feature, and then expand on the benefit, showing the prospect why it matters to them personally.

Remember, people are not so concerned about every feature that a product might have. They want to know if it will make their life easier, or resolve their pain, or allow them to have more time to spend with their family.

Third, your script must have stopping-off points.

If you make a powerful statement, and then another powerful statement, and then yet another powerful statement, by the time you've made the third powerful statement, they've all started to blend in with one another, and they lose their power. This is why a well-written script has an abundance of *stopping-off points*, where the prospect will interact with you and affirm that you're still on the same page.

In other words, after you make a powerful statement, you want to lock it down by asking the prospect a simple yes-or-no question, such as: "You follow me so far?" or "Make sense?" or "Are you with me?" By doing this, not only do you keep the prospect engaged in the conversation but you also get them into the habit of saying yes, which creates consistency.

In addition, these little stopping-off points serve as periodic rapport checks. For example, if you say to your prospect "Make sense so far?" and they reply "Yes," then you're in rapport; however, if they reply, "No," then you're *out* of rapport, and you can't move forward in the script until you've gotten to the bottom of things. If you do, then your prospect will be thinking: "This guy couldn't care less about what I'm saying; he's just looking to make a commission."

So, instead of moving forward, you're going to loop back and give your prospect a little more information that relates to that topic, and then ask them again if things make sense so far. Once they say yes—which they almost always will in this case—you can then safely move forward.

Fourth, write in the spoken word, not grammatically correct English.

You want to be speaking in a casual manner, using layman's terms, not in formal English or using overly technical lingo.

In other words, when you read the script, the writing itself should sound totally natural, with the prose written in a manner as if you were speaking to a friend and trying to connect with them emotionally, not just logically.

Now, on the flip side, remember that you still have to sound like an expert. So there's a balance to be struck. It's not all like: "Hey, buh, buh, buh. We are like, these, them, dos and don'ts"—like a Brooklyn guy who's not educated, right? You still want to sound educated, like an expert. But don't try to talk above your prospect by using too many technical buzz phrases; that's about as surefire of a way I know to get someone to tune out.

Rather, you want to use colloquialisms whenever possible, and use contractions to keep your prose sounding natural and snappy. But you can never forget that your commitment to sounding natural is always in the context of being perceived as an expert.

Fifth, your script must flow perfectly.

When I write a new script, I always go through at least four or five drafts before I lock in a final version. This gives me a chance to test the script out—first by reading it out loud to myself, to identify any obvious glitches in the rhythm or flow of the various language patterns. For example, are there any tongue-twisters in the prose or sentences that are out of balance, in terms of the number of syllables or beats they contain? Are there any awkward transitions that need to be smoothed out?

I will then rewrite the script, fixing the glitches I found, and then repeat the process again, until I'm absolutely certain that every single word flows like silk.

By doing that, I ensure that even a rookie salesperson can use the script and sound totally awesome. To that end, one of the key elements that I always make it a point to focus on very closely is balance, in terms of the number of syllables and the number of beats in each sentence.

You see, if a sentence is out of balance, the human ear will immediately sense that something doesn't sound right, and after just a few repetitions, it will tune out.

Sixth, your scripts must be honest and ethical.

When you're writing your script, you should ask yourself, with every single sentence: "Is everything I'm saying 100 percent accurate? Am I coming from a place of integrity? Am I coming from a place of ethics?

"Or am I starting to exaggerate the facts? Am I misleading people? Am I making any material omissions of fact?"

I'm the first one to admit that I wrote some scripts back in the early days that I'm not particularly proud of. It's not that they were full of lies, but there were some serious omissions of fact, which ended up painting a very skewed picture of things.

So, please, for your own sake, I want you to make sure that your scripts are not only 100 percent accurate but also come from a place of ethics and integrity—meaning, you need to have a zero tolerance policy in place when it comes to things like lying and exaggerating and misleading and omitting, or anything else that wouldn't pass the so-called smell test.

In addition, for those of you who are in management, or if you're an owner of the company, always remember that if you hand your sales force a script that's riddled with lies and exaggerations, they will most certainly know it—and the consequences will be disastrous.

For starters, passing out an unethical script is tantamount to giving your sales force corporate approval to go out and rape and pillage the village. You see, as your salespeople are out there banging away on the phone or knocking on doors in the field, they're lying and exaggerating or omitting key facts every time they make a sales presentation, and it will quickly seep into your entire corporate culture and poison it.

In fact, before long, your sales force will spiral completely out of control—making up bolder and bolder lies and wilder and wilder exaggerations with each passing day, as they become more and more desensitized to their own lack of ethics, which started with you!

The bottom line is that you can't be half-pregnant when it comes to ethics, so any notion you have that you can hand out a deceitful script and not have it ultimately destroy your entire corporate culture is foolish. Your scripts need to be accurate, compliant, and reflective of your corporate culture, which is one of ethics and integrity.

And they also need to be sexy as all hell!

Remember, these things are not mutually exclusive: your script can be sexy and compelling and still 100 percent ethical.

To sum it up, your script should be the truth well told.

Seventh, remember the overarching equation of energy in, benefits out.

The moment before a prospect makes a buying decision, they run a lightning-fast equation through their mind that weighs the difference between the total amount of energy they'll have to expend, in order to go through the closing process and receive your product, against the total value of all the amazing benefits you've promised them, both immediately and in the future.

To that end, if the value of the expected benefits exceeds the total projected energy expenditure, then the prospect's brain will issue an all clear sign and they can then decide whether or not they want to buy. Conversely, if the value of the expected benefits is *less* than the projected energy expenditure, then a red flag goes up, eliminating any chance of the prospect buying until you've satisfied the equation.

The name of this equation is *energy in, benefits out*, and it comes into play each time you ask for the order—including when you respond to buy signals during the back half of the sale.

This principle doesn't even register with the prospect's conscious mind until a microsecond after you've asked for the order, at which point it springs into action—instructing their inner monologue to pose a simple, yet *very* pointed question, namely: *At the end of the day, is it really worth it?*

In other words, from a sober, logical perspective, is the sum total of all the benefits I expect to receive greater than the sum total of all the energy I'll have to expend in order to receive them?

Now, what you need to understand here is that although a positive outcome to this equation doesn't necessarily mean that your prospect will buy, a negative outcome to this equation means that they definitely *won't* buy. This is not *forever*, but until you get another chance to ask for the order again, at which point you'll adhere to a set of simple yet extremely effective principles that will ensure you end up on the right side of this equation.

Let me quickly lay these principles out for you, using our trusted subjects Bill Peterson and John Smith as examples.

So let's say Bill Peterson just finished making a kick-ass sales presentation to John Smith, during which he explained to him his product's myriad benefits and why they're a perfect solution to the challenges Mr. Smith is facing, to which Mr. Smith completely agreed—giving Bill all the right signals throughout the entire sales presentation.

So, all Bill has to do *now* is lay out a closing scenario, explaining the various steps that Mr. Smith needs to take to get the ball rolling, and then ask him for the order.

To that end, Bill says to Mr. Smith:

"Now, John, here's what I need you to do: first, I need you to give me your full name, your social security number, your address, your driver's license number, and then I want you to go to the post office, get a special first-class stamp, then take your license to a copy machine, make a copy of it, then run it over to the notary and get it notarized, and then run to the bank to get a certified check . . ." And then only after Mr. Smith has jumped through a dozen hoops and a ring of fire can he get all the amazing benefits that Bill Peterson promised him that his product would deliver.

Obviously, I'm exaggerating a bit here, but not by all that much. Most companies really miss the boat on this one—using closing scenarios that require the prospect to expend so much energy that they've made it close to impossible for them to end up on the right side of this equation.

By the way, never forget that money is basically nothing more than stored energy. In essence, you expend energy by engaging in some type of work, for which you receive money in return. Now, of course, *some* of that money ends up being used for basic living expenses—food, shelter, clothing, medical expenses, general bill paying—and the rest of it you deposit in the bank, where it represents stored energy that can be unleashed in any way you wish, at a moment's notice.

In consequence, when you ask someone to take action and send you their hard-earned money, you're asking them to expend their stored energy, so you want to be sure to offset that energy expenditure by highlighting all the valuable benefits that they're going to receive in return.

In essence, you want to crystallize the fact that once they say yes they're going to receive a massive number of valuable benefits, and the amount of energy they'll have to expend will be considerably lower.

By the way, one company that does this just about as well as a company can possibly do it is Amazon. With their one-click buying option, they've made it so ridiculously easy for a customer to receive a product's benefits that you start to feel that it's simply too much of a hassle to buy from anyone else.

Even *more* telling, what Amazon has found is that if their customers are forced to click even one more time, to go to a different landing page, they will lose a major percentage of their buyers; and if a customer has to click a *third* time, their conversion rate drops through the floor. That's how important this equation is to people making a positive buying decision.

Let's go back to the example of Bill Peterson and John Smith—except, this time, let's change the language pattern to reflect a very different type of closing scenario:

"Now, John, getting started here is very, very simple. It's just a question of your name, some basic information, and then we handle everything else for you over on this end. And when you combine *that* with [benefit #1] and [benefit #2] and [benefit #3], then, believe me, John, the only problem you're going to have is that you didn't buy more. Sound fair enough?"

That's a very low energy in, massive benefits out close, and it can be easily adapted to any industry.

However, one thing I need to point out is that sometimes you're going to find yourself in a situation where the process or the product you're selling is actually not all that simple to get started. An example might be in banking or mortgages, where there are hoops to jump through and a lot of paperwork.

So, while you can't say something is simple when it's actually very complicated, you can still make it clear to your prospect that you will do everything in your power to make the process as simple as possible for them.

Now, before we move on, let's quickly go through the process of how to handle buy signals when they arise in the back half of the sale. In other words, as your prospect starts to become more and more certain about the Three Tens, they will start sending you signals that they are interested in buying, in the form of leading questions about the closing process.

For example, the prospect might say, "How much did you say it would run me?" or "How long will it take until I receive the product?" or "How long until I start to see results?" Those are just a few examples of the more common buy signals.

Let's say you've already asked for the order for the first time and you're in the middle of running a looping pattern, and your prospect suddenly asks, "What was the price on that again?" To which you reply, "Oh, it's only three thousand dollars," and you say no more.

Alas, you just committed sales hara-kiri.

Why?

Simply put, you've just created a scenario where there's $3,000 worth of energy going in and zero benefits coming out, not because those benefits don't exist—in point of fact, they do—but because you simply forgot to remind the prospect of them at the same time you asked them to tap into their energy reserves.

In other words, the fact that you laid out the benefits three or four minutes ago when you asked for the order for the first time has no bearing on the energy in, benefits out equation a few minutes later, when your prospect gave you a buy signal.

Put another way, human beings have extremely short memories when it comes to the balancing effect of benefits. In consequence, you need to restate those benefits again, albeit more quickly and succinctly, but you still need to state them every time you bring up the expenditure of energy.

To that end, the proper way to have responded to the buy signal "What was the price on that again?" is as follows:

"It's a cash outlay of only three thousand dollars, and let me quickly tell you exactly what you're going to get for that: you're going to get [benefit #1] and [benefit #2] and [benefit #3], and again, like I said before, getting started is very, very simple, so believe me, if you do even *half* as well as the rest of my clients in this program, then the only problem you'll have is that I didn't call you six months ago and get you started then. Sound fair enough?"

And *that's* how you close.

I used the word "cash outlay" as a reframer, instead of cost; I used the word "only" as a minimizer, in relation to the $3,000; I then quickly reminded the prospect of three major benefits, to balance out the $3,000 energy expenditure; and then I reiterated the simplicity of getting started and transitioned into a soft close—using my tri-tonal pattern of absolute certainty, collapsing into utter sincerity, and then moving into the reasonable man tone, as I said my last three words: "Sound fair enough?"

Then I shut up.

And eighth, a Straight Line script is part of a series of scripts.

In fact, there might be as many as five or six different scripts that take you through from the open to the close. For example, you'll have a script that starts with those all-important first four seconds, and then includes your qualifying questions and your transition. Second, you'll have a script that starts with the main body of your presentation and ends with you asking for the order for the first time. Third, you'll have a series of rebuttal scripts that include the well-thought-out answers you've prepared to the various common objections you're going to hear. And fourth, you'll have a series of looping scripts that will include the various language patterns that will allow you to loop back into the sale, in order to move your prospect to higher and higher levels of certainty.

This leads us to an *extremely* important aspect of the sales process that's going to have a major impact on how you construct and deliver each of the above scripts, in terms of their length, their breadth, and how much time you have to spend repeating yourself in order to refresh your prospect's recollection.

What I'm referring to here is the issue of the type of call system you're using—meaning, how many times do you plan on speaking to your prospect before you ask them the first time for the order? Once? Twice? Three times? Four times?

Whichever the case, the logic behind using a sales system with two or more calls is that each prior call, whether it's in person or over the phone, serves as a springboard for entering the *next* call in a tighter state of rapport and with greater insight into the prospect's needs and pain points, as a result of the intelligence you gathered on the previous calls. And it's given *the prospect* a chance to review whatever documents or links you've sent, or to do his or her own research in order to increase their level of certainty about each of the Three Tens.

To that end, there isn't much you can do on three calls that you couldn't have done on two; so whenever I consult for a company that's using a three-call system, I always make them at least *test* a two-call system, in conjunction, of course, with teaching them the rest of the

Straight Line System, which is what I was hired to do in the first place. And, in the end, rare indeed are the tests that don't prove the benefits of using the two-call system, if for no other reason than how difficult it is to get in touch with same prospects three times within the confines of the outer limits of your sales cycle.

In other words, every product or service will have its own predetermined sales cycle that has a set number of days between calls. At a certain point, when a prospect has exceeded the outer limit for the number of days between calls, the lead goes into a dead pile, which eventually gets redistributed to someone else in the sales force after the appropriate amount of time—usually three to six months, or maybe even a year; any longer than that and the close rate drop becomes negligible.

This circumvents the self-defeating behavior of chasing after the same prospect again and again, which is par for the course for a non–Straight Line salesperson, even after it would be painfully obvious to any other human being that the prospect is ducking their call when it pops up on the prospect's caller ID.

The same goes for a four-call system, although they're so counterintuitive (even to a poorly trained sales manager) that whenever I *do* run into one, there's usually a valid reason why the sale has been dragged out. Most of the time, it has to do with the reality of having to deal with multiple decision-makers, which causes a salesperson to have to work their way up the ladder—closing one decision-maker at a time, until eventually getting the final decision-maker to sign off on the deal.

The other common reason is a particular product requiring that the buyer commit a significant amount of their own resources—either time, money, manpower, or all three—to integrate the new product into their current business; so, before they sign on the dotted line, there's a significant amount of forethought and strategic planning required.

For example, in a four-call-system, a successful outcome for the third call might be your prospect agreeing to sign a letter of intent and, in the cases where it's necessary, a nondisclosure agreement, so the prospect and their team can take a closer look at the *inner workings* of your product—a process formally known as "due diligence"—to make sure that it's everything you've cracked it up to be.

In addition, this is *also* the point in the sale where lawyers from *both* sides tend to get involved—going back and forth as they review each other's changes, as they take what started off as a simple, straightforward agreement and complicate it to the point of madness while racking up massive legal fees in the process.

Now, to be clear, while most lawyers are reasonably honest, there are still a lot of chronic over-billers out there, so be careful—*especially* if your commission is tied to the overall profitability of the deal! If that's the case, then you definitely want to make sure that someone competent goes through every invoice with a fine-tooth comb and negotiates out anything that looks even slightly suspicious (because this is definitely one of those cases where if there's smoke, there's fire!).

Anyway, moving along, once your prospect's team has given the thumbs-up from their due diligence, and the lawyers have extracted the appropriate amount of flesh from everyone's bones, then you have the chance to truly close the deal, which usually entails the signing of a definitive agreement, or contract, and the exchange of a predetermined amount of money.

The most important thing to remember throughout this entire process is that until a definitive agreement gets signed and money changes hands, the deal is not closed, which means you need to keep in touch with the prospect and do whatever you can to keep the Three Tens at the highest level possible. This includes sending your prospect testimonials from other satisfied clients; articles from trade journals, newspapers, and magazines that reinforce the idea that the prospect made the right decision; and occasional emails and regular schmooze calls to make sure that you stay in tight rapport as the process drags on.

I cannot overestimate how dramatically this will reduce the number of deals that end up falling out of bed during the waiting period. And while it usually takes anywhere from four to six weeks to complete the process, it *can* drag on for up to three months, if those special types of lawyers are involved and the prospect isn't under any time pressure to close the deal.

Nonetheless, as long as you continue to keep your prospect's level of certainty as high as possible, then things should end up okay, and you'll close the majority of deals that make it this far and get your commission, which had better be substantial, considering how long the deal took and all the trouble you had to go through to get it to actually close.

Just how substantial is impossible to say without knowing all the details, but suffice to say that if your commission is not in the thousands of dollars for a deal that took six months to close, then you better be getting a hefty base salary to make up for it.

But, again, there are simply too many variables in play—the country you live in, what's considered normal in the industry, your opportunity for advancement within the company you work for, how much enjoyment you get out of what you're doing—for me to give you an answer on compensation that's anything more than an educated guess.

More importantly, though, you need to make sure that during the waiting period all your communications to your "almost" new client come from a position of strength—meaning that, as far as you're concerned, the deal is already closed and the communication you're sending is from the perspective of building a long-term relationship and doing more business in the future. Otherwise, you'll come off as being desperate, and it will end up having the reverse effect.

But other than those two examples, anything more than a three-call system will be the result of a flawed sales process being administered by an equally flawed sales manager, who's sitting idly by and watching a team of what are *always* inexperienced salespeople banging their heads against the wall, trying to get through to the same person four times before they get around to asking for the order. After all, if there was anyone experienced on the sales force, they would first suggest, and then ultimately demand, that they be allowed to collapse the number of calls to three or less; and just so you're aware, that demand is almost always accompanied by a sales force–wide revolt led by the experienced salesperson, who is preying on the cloud of desperation that hangs over an underperforming sales force like sarin gas, poisoning their hearts and minds and breaking their collective spirit.

In light of that, whether you're the owner, the sales manager, or just a salesperson in the sales force, you need to pay extremely close attention to the number of calls in your sales cycle, with an eye toward collapsing it to as few calls as possible. The way to safely and effectively do this is to eliminate one call from the cycle at a time, until you've reached the point where a decrease in your percentage-closing rate isn't offset by a greater number of total closed deals (due to the large increase in the number of sales calls made to close deals, as opposed to setting up the next call).

The Power of Language Patterns

As I explained in Chapter 2, the Straight Line is basically a visual representation of the perfect sale—where everything you say and everything you do and every case you make as to why your prospect should buy from you is met with an unequivocal yes from the prospect, right up to the moment where you ask them for the order and they agree to close.

In addition, every word that escapes your lips has been specifically designed to feed into one overarching goal, which is to increase your prospect's level of certainty for each of the Three Tens to the highest level possible, a 10 on the certainty scale.

Now, in terms of the order in which you go about creating certainty, you're always going to follow the same protocol, which is:

* **The product first**

* **You, the salesperson second**

* **And the company that stands behind the product third**

In terms of the split between logic and emotion, you're always going to build airtight logical cases first and airtight emotional cases second. Why?

Quite simply, by making the airtight logical case *first*, you satisfy your prospect's bullshit detector, which then frees them up to be moved emotionally.

The way you're going to accomplish this is through a series of expertly constructed Straight Line scripts—ensuring that you know *exactly* what to say before you have to say it; and embedded in these scripts are going to be language patterns, which are bite-sized chunks of expertly crafted information, each of which has a specific goal in mind.

For example, there are patterns designed to create logical certainty and there are patterns designed to create emotional certainty; there are patterns designed to create certainty for each of the Three Tens, and there is a pattern to lower someone's action threshold and one to add on pain.

In short, there is a pattern for everything.

In the front half of the sale, your language patterns serve as anchors for each step of the syntax, and they're an important aspect of ensuring

a successful outcome. In the back half of the sale, your language patterns serve as the very foundation for the entire looping process, and
everything you say will revolve around them.

In your opening pattern, you're simply introducing yourself, your
company, and explaining the reason for your call, while using tonality
and body language to establish yourself as an expert, so you can take
control of the conversation and begin moving your prospect down the
straight line, from the open to the close. Here are the basic rules for creating a powerful introduction. We'll assume an outbound phone call:

- **Be enthusiastic right from the start.**

- **Always speak in the familiar. For example, you wouldn't say,
  "Hi, is Mr. Jones there?" You would say, "Hi, is John there?"**

- **Introduce yourself and your company in the first couple of
  sentences, and then restate the name of your company a second
  time within the first couple of sentences.**

- **Use power words, like "dramatically," "explosive," "fastest growing," "most well respected." Power words go a very long way
  to capturing someone's attention and establishing yourself as
  an expert.**

- **Use your justifiers (I went through these in Chapter 10).**

- **Ask for permission to begin the qualification process.**

Your next pattern is going to allow you to smoothly transition into
the intelligence-gathering phase, and it will include asking your prospect for permission to ask questions, as well as all the questions you

intend on asking your prospect, laid out in exactly the right order, with notations attached that indicate which tonality will be applied in order to ensure that you get the most comprehensive response. And, of course, at the same time, you'll make it a point to be actively listening to each of your prospect's responses, to ensure that you are building massive rapport on both a conscious and unconscious level.

Here are some sample big picture questions that can be used in virtually any industry:

What do you like or dislike about your current supplier?

Typically, a prospect will have a current source or be using a similar product already, and you aren't the first person to try to sell them a new product of this nature. This is a very powerful question.

What is your biggest headache with your business?

You have to be *very* careful with your tonality here, as this is your first direct attempt at identifying your prospect's pain. For example, if you flippantly say, "So, John, what's your biggest headache with this? Come on, *tell* me!" it says that you don't give a shit. The proper tonality here should convey sincerity, concern, and a desire to help resolve John's pain; and when he starts talking about it, you want to amplify that pain by asking the following questions:

"How long has this been going on?" "Do you see this getting better or worse?" "How do you see yourself in two years?" "How has it affected your health or your family?"

In essence, you want to make sure that you make your prospect talk about their pain. These types of questions will have a powerful impact on opening the prospect's mind to receiving information, which they will now measure against their pain.

What would be your ideal program if you could design it?

Now, this question works extremely well in some industries and doesn't apply to others. The key here is to use a logic-based tonality, as if you were a scientist talking, versus a tonality of empathy.

Of all the factors that we have just spoken about, what is the most important to you?

You definitely want to find out your prospect's highest need, as this is the one that you'll typically have to fill to push the prospect over the top.

Have I asked about everything that's important to you?

Your customer will think more of you, not less of you, if you ask this, so long as you have done a professional job up to that point. You could also say, "Is there anything that I have missed? Is there any way that I can tailor this solution for you?"

This takes us to the end of your introduction—where you'll transition into the main body of your sales presentation—so let's do a quick recap of the various language patterns:

1 When you introduce yourself, remember to speak in the familiar and to always sound upbeat and enthusiastic.

2 The next pattern is going to be to get their response of "I'm okay." "If you recall, we met last Thursday night at the Marriott," or "If you recall, you sent in a postcard a few weeks back," or "We've been reaching out to people in your area . . ." In short, you are trying to link up this call with the time you first met your prospect, or when they took an action, like filling out a postcard or clicking on a website.

3 This next pattern is extremely important and is the reason for the call, your *justifier*. In essence, your justifier creates a valid reason to be calling today, and it will dramatically increase your compliance rate.

4 From here you get into the qualifying portion of your script, and you start by asking for permission to ask questions. This is another example of using a justifier, this time with the word "so." "Just a couple of quick questions *so* I don't waste your time." This gives a reason why you need to ask the prospect questions, and that reason is so you don't waste their time. You always want to ask for permission to qualify.

5 The last part of your open is always a transition. "Based on everything you said to me, this is a perfect fit for you." This should be an anchor for you; you should know it by heart.

When it comes to the main body of your presentation, I can't give you exact language patterns, as they vary too greatly from industry to industry. However, that being said, when I'm hired by a company to do a sales training, I make each salesperson create three or four language patterns for each of the Three Tens, and then I *pool* them all together and pick the best of the patterns to create one master script.

If possible, I strongly recommend that you do that yourself—recruiting other salespeople in your office to go through this exercise with you as a group.

To that end, let me give you a head start by providing you with a handful of powerful tips and guidelines for creating language patterns for the body and the close.

1 The moment you finish the above transition, your first words in the main body should be the exact name of your product,

process, program, or service you're offering. Here's an example of this that I wrote for the movie *The Wolf of Wall Street*:

"Name of the company . . . Aerotyne International. It's a cutting-edge, high-tech firm out of the Midwest, awaiting imminent patent approval on a next generation of radar detectors that have both huge military and civilian applications."

2 The next language pattern should be no more than one or two paragraphs and be focused on a benefit that directly fills the clients need. (Only mention that feature.) If possible, try to use comparisons and metaphors to illustrate your point, as they are far more effective than facts and figures alone. In addition, if you can ethically link the above pattern to a trustworthy person or institution, like a Warren Buffett or J. P. Morgan, then do it. (Also, check to see if your company knows of any high-profile people who have used your product and liked it.) The bottom line is that anytime you can leverage the credibility of a respected person or institution, you should try to bring it into your presentation.

3 After you're done with the pattern, you should say, "You follow me so far?" or "Make sense?" You can only move forward after the prospect says yes; otherwise you'll break rapport and enter the death zone. But once they agree with you—*boom!*—you've completed one full language pattern.

4 Now, repeat steps two and three one more time—and then one more time again, but no more than that, or you'll run the risk of overwhelming the client. Always remember, you're framing, not front-loading!

5 As you're transitioning into your close, you should try to create some type of urgency—meaning, why the customer needs to buy now. If you're in an industry where there's not a lot of inherent urgency, then try to at least use tonal scarcity to imply urgency. But don't create false urgency; that's not okay.

6 Moving from the main body to the close, we start with a transitional pattern that explains how simple it is to get the buying process started. (This is your energy in, benefits out equation.)

7 Then you directly ask for the order, with no beating around the bush. The reason I'm highlighting this is that after spending the last ten years training sales forces all around the world, I've found that the vast majority of salespeople don't ask for the order very much. Either they dance around it, or they leave it open-ended, as if they're hoping the prospect will just come right out and say they want to buy it. In point of fact, most studies peg the optimum number of times that a salesperson should ask for the order as somewhere between five and seven times.

Personally, however, I strongly disagree, and I think that number has more to do with poorly trained salespeople going through the closing process in a wildly inefficient way. Three or four times should be more than enough when you're using the Straight Line System. Remember, this is not about pressuring people into making bad decisions; this is about using the Straight Line System to create massive certainty in the mind of your prospect, on both a logical and emotional level, and then asking for the order in a low-pressure, graceful way.

Here's a typical language pattern for a close:

"Give me one shot, and believe me, if I'm even half-right,
the only problem you'll have is that I didn't call you six
months ago and get you started then. Sound fair enough?"

So, there you have it: the basic framework for constructing world-class scripts that set you up to close a massive number of deals.

Once you've gone through the script-building process and you've finalized your draft, there are only two things left to do:

Training and *drilling*.

I can't even begin to tell you how massive the payoff will be if you take the time to read your script out loud, and keep practicing and practicing until you get to a level of unconscious competence where you literally know your script by heart.

Now, I don't expect you to get this perfect the first time out, but what I will tell you is that script writing has a very strong Good Enough Factor, which means that even if you're just *okay* at writing scripts, it will still dramatically increase your closing rate.

To that end, one question I always get asked is, "When should I use my script?" And my answer to that is, "ALWAYS!"

You should *always* use a script, whether you're selling in person or on the phone. *How do you use a script in person?* you're wondering.

Very simple—you have it memorized.

Like I said, I want to know my scripts so well that I move past the point of the actual words. Remember, 10 percent of human communication is words; the other 90 percent is tonality and body language. By memorizing my script, I free up my conscious mind to focus on the 90 percent.

So I urge you to keep reading your scripts back to yourself, to make sure all the language patterns and transitions are absolutely seamless. It takes a bit of time, but I promise you that it's well worth it.

12

THE ART AND SCIENCE OF LOOPING

SINCE THE DAY I INVENTED THE STRAIGHT LINE SYSTEM, ONE OF the core principles that I've been drilling into the hearts and minds of all the people I've trained is that the sale doesn't truly begin until *after* your prospect hits you with the first objection; only *then* do you have the chance to finally roll up your sleeves and earn your paycheck.

To that end, regardless of what product you're selling, there are only three possible ways that your prospect can respond the first time you ask them for the order.

They can say:

* *Yes*—meaning, the deal is closed and it's time to break out the paperwork and collect payment.

In essence, these are the *lay-down sales* that I spoke about in Chapter 2, where the prospects are basically *pre-sold* before they enter the sales encounter. As salespeople, we love getting them, but, from a practical standpoint, they're far too rare to put any stock in them as an expected outcome.

The key here is to manage your expectations.

You want to appreciate lay-downs when they come, without ever *expecting* them to come. This ensures that you'll enter the back half of the sale with the same level of certainty and with the same positive mind-set that you had when you entered the front half of the sale.

- *No*—meaning, the prospect is definitely *not interested* and it's time to end the sales encounter and move on to the next prospect.

Now, in reality, if you've been correctly following the steps in the Straight Line Syntax, then you should almost never get hit with an outright "I'm not interested" at this point in the sale. After all, you will have already weeded out the prospects who indicated that during the intelligence-gathering phase.

In other words, the only prospects you should be presenting to at this point are those whose answers to your intelligence-gathering questions dictated that they not only were interested in your product but also needed your product and could afford your product.

So it completely defies logic that someone who ticked all those boxes would suddenly do a complete one-eighty after you just presented them with a series of benefits that were a perfect match for them.

In terms of the exact percentages, you shouldn't expect to get hit with a flat-out no more than 1 or 2 percent of the time, which is right on par with your lay-downs.

- Or *maybe*—meaning, the prospect is sitting on the fence and can still go either way. *Maybe* consists of all the common objections that salespeople typically get hit with during the back half of the sale. In total, there are somewhere between twelve and fourteen of them, although about half are just simple variations of two.

I've already listed them in Chapter 2, but for the sake of convenience, and also to refresh your recollection, here are the most common ones again:

"Let me think about it"; "Let me call you back"; "Send me some information"; "I'm not liquid right now"; "I have another source [or supplier or broker] I work with"; "It's a bad time of year [including it's tax time, it's summer vacation time, it's Christmastime, it's the end of our fiscal year]"; and "I need to speak to someone else [which includes my spouse, my lawyer, my accountant, my business partner, my financial advisor]."

The Art of Deflection

Let's say you're a stockbroker cold-calling wealthy investors, trying to persuade them to open up a new account at your brokerage firm, XYZ Securities. The stock that you're recommending as an opening trade is Microsoft, which is currently trading at $30 per share, and the firm minimum for opening up a new account is $3,000, or one hundred shares of Microsoft.

Using a standard two-call system, your closing rate is 30 percent—meaning, you close three out of every ten prospects who you can get on the phone a second time—and 90 percent of that 30 percent end up buying after your third or fourth time asking for the order.

From start to finish, it takes you approximately three minutes to go through the front half of the sale and between ten and fifteen minutes to go through the back half of the sale; and while the front half of the sale might strike you as being unusually short, what you need to remember here is that, with a two-call system, virtually all of your intelligence gathering and initial rapport-building gets completed on the first call, giving you a significant head start on the second call.

That is not to say that you don't have to spend at least *some* amount of time reengaging your prospect when you begin the second call; but that entire process should take no more than a minute, as opposed to the five to *seven* minutes it takes to complete an initial call.

Specifically, the reengagement process consists of you leading your prospect, Bill Peterson, through the following steps:

1 Start your introduction by greeting Bill by his first name, and then quickly reintroduce yourself—stating your first and last name, the name of your company, and its location—and ask Bill how he's doing today. Remember, from your very first word, your tonality must be positive and upbeat, with a *hint* of bottled enthusiasm slipping out around the edges.

2 Remind him that you two spoke a few days or a few weeks ago, and that you emailed him a bit of information on your company. Do not—*I repeat, do not*—ask him if he actually *received* the information or had a chance to review it, as there's an excellent possibility that he'll say "no" to at least one of those questions, which gives him an easy exit ramp out of the encounter. The way to avoid this is to simply ask him if the conversation "rings a bell," to which he will almost always reply with a yes.

3 Once he does, then briefly explain to him how the last time you spoke, he asked you to give him a call the next time an extraordinary investment idea came across your desk.

4 If he replies no, then act a bit surprised, but chalk it up to the fact that he must get a ton of calls and emails each day, and then assure him that you did, in fact, speak to him, and that you did, in fact, email him some information; but there's no need to worry, as it was just a bit of background on your company. Then complete step three—reminding him that he

asked you to call him the next time you had an investment idea.

5 Explain how something just came across your desk and that it's one of the best things you've seen in quite some time now, and if he has sixty seconds, you'd like to share the idea with him.

6 Complete your introduction by saying *"Got a minute?"* using the reasonable man tone.*

Here is how the reengagement process looks in script form, showing a prospect's typical responses as well:

You: Hi, is Bill there?

Your Prospect: Yeah, this is Bill.

You: Hey, Bill! It's John Smith, calling from XYZ Securities, on Wall Street. How you doing today?

Your Prospect: I'm okay.

You: Okay, great! Now, Bill, if you recall, we spoke a few weeks back, and I emailed you a bit of information on my company, XYZ Securities, along with some links to a few of our recent stock recommendations. Does that ring a bell?

Your Prospect: Uh, yeah, I *think* so.

You: Okay, great! Now, Bill, the last time we spoke, I promised to get back to you when I came across an investment idea that had huge upside potential with very little downside risk. Well, the *reason* for the call today is that something *just* came across my desk, and it's perhaps the best thing I've seen in the last

---

* Go to www.jordanbelfort.com/tonality to listen to the tonality.

six months. If you have sixty seconds, I'd like to share the idea with you. You got a minute?

And that's it.

From there, you're going to smoothly transition into the main body of your presentation, adhering to the rules and guidelines laid out in the previous chapter, on script building, and then you'll close out the front half of the sale by *directly* asking for the order for the first time, in no uncertain terms—meaning, there's no beating around the bush or *kind of* asking for the order; you're flat-out asking for it, saying something along the lines of: "Bill, here's what I want you to do: pick up a block of ten thousand shares of Microsoft at thirty dollars a share. It's a cash outlay of three hundred thousand dollars, or half that on margin . . ." And then complete your closing pattern.

Now, in reality, this is a far bigger investment than you expect your prospect to ultimately make; however, by asking for such a large commitment on the first go-round, you now have the opportunity to incrementally lower that amount with each new closing attempt—timing the reductions so that, on your final closing attempt, you're asking your prospect for the firm's minimum commitment for opening a new account.

In general sales parlance, we refer to this strategy as a step-down sale, and it can be a powerful closing tool for products where you can easily ratchet up or ratchet down the amount of the purchase. For example, in Bill's case, when you ask him for the order for the *second* time, you would step him down from ten thousand shares to five thousand shares, which reduces the energy-*in* aspect of the closing equation by 50 percent, after you just increased the benefits-*out* side of the equation during your follow-up presentation. This creates an extremely powerful one-two punch that will significantly increase your closing rate. And, of course, on your third closing attempt, you would step down to a thousand shares . . . and then down to five hundred shares on your fourth attempt, going all the way down to whatever the firm's minimum is for opening up a new account.

Now, remember, on your initial closing attempt, you fully expect to be hit with one of the common objections, so your inner monologue should be saying, "Ahhh, just as expected! A smoke screen for uncertainty! It's time to roll up my sleeves and earn my paycheck!" In terms of which objection your prospect chooses, it doesn't even matter, because you're going to respond to all the common objections in exactly the same way.

For example, let's say Bill replies, "It sounds interesting. Let me think about it."

To that, you'll answer with the standard Straight Line response to an initial objection, which is: **"I hear what you're saying, Bill, but let me ask you a question: Does the idea make sense to you? Do you *like* the idea?"**

Similarly, if Bill had said, "I need to speak to my accountant," then you would've said, "I hear what you're saying, Bill, but let me ask you a question: Does the idea make sense to you? Do you *like* the idea?"

And, once again, if he had said, "It's a bad time of year," then you would've said, "I hear what you're saying, Bill, but let me just ask you a question: Does the idea make sense to you? Do you *like* the idea?"

In other words, no matter which of the twelve to fourteen common objections your prospect initially hits you with, you are always going to answer in exactly the same way.

You're going to say:

"I hear what you're saying, Bill, but let me ask you a question: Does the idea make sense to you? Do you *like* the idea?"

Now, notice how, rather than directly answering his objection, you deflected it instead.

Specifically, you acknowledged the fact that you heard what Bill said to you—to ensure that he didn't feel ignored, which would cause a break in rapport—and then you shifted the conversation in a more productive direction, which was to find out where he stood on the certainty scale for the first of the Three Tens, which is your product.

In Straight Line parlance, we refer to this process as *deflection*, and it comprises step number six of the Straight Line Syntax. In essence, when you deflect a prospect's initial objection, you're avoiding answering it head-on by using a two-step process:

Step one consists of a simple, five-word language pattern—*I hear what you're saying*—which you've infused with the *reasonable man* tonality.*

Your words let the prospect know that you've heard his objection (and, hence, you're not ignoring him), and your tonality lets the prospect know that you fully respect his right to feel that way, which ensures that you remain in very tight rapport.

Step two consists of another simple language pattern—*Let me ask you a question: Does the idea makes sense to you? Do you* like *the idea?*—which you've infused with the *money-aside* tonality.

So, again, your words are redirecting the conversation to a far more productive track, which, in this particular case, is to ascertain Bill's current level of certainty about Microsoft being a good buy right now; and your tonality ensures that he doesn't feel pressured by your question—that if he admits that he *likes* your product, you're not going to use his admission against him to pressure him to buy. After all, if he feels that way, then he'll significantly tone down his level of enthusiasm as he responds, which is the last thing you want your prospect to be doing at this point.

Why?

---

*   Go to www.jordanbelfort.com/tonality to listen to the tonality.

Well, quite simply, while a *basic* yes is enough to move forward during the front half of the sale, you need an *enthusiastic* yes to move forward during the back half of the sale.

The reason for this is that the level of enthusiasm of your prospect's yes is going to serve as your primary means for measuring his level of certainty for each of the Three Tens.

For example, suppose that, in response to deflecting Bill's initial objection, he replied in an ambivalent tone: "Yeah, it sounds pretty good."

Now, here's a very important question: Where does Bill's response—including his ambivalent tone—place him on the certainty scale? Is he at a 3? A 5? A 9? A 10?

Well, he's *clearly* not at a 10, *right?*

After all, when your prospect is at a 10, you'll definitely know it. His response will sound something like this: "Oh, *yeah, absolutely!* It makes *total* sense to me. I love the idea!" In essence, his positive bias will be so strong that his words and his tonality are dead giveaways for his ultra-high level of certainty.

The same is true of a 1 on the certainty scale, albeit in the exact opposite direction. His response, in this case, will sound something like this: "No, not at all. I think it's one of the stupidest ideas I've ever heard," and his tone will be one of utter disgust.

While the levels in between are a bit more challenging to hit on the nose, he's *clearly* not at a 2 or a 3, as either one has far more negative emotion attached to its response than Bill's did; conversely, he's clearly not at an 8 or a 9, as either of those levels has far more *positive* emotion attached.

So, where is he, then?

Where is Bill on the certainty scale based on his response?

Well, I wasn't kidding when I said it's a bit harder to hit those middle levels directly on the nose; but, still, based on his words and their accompanying tonality, I would say he's somewhere around a 5 or a 6, although maybe he's at a 4, but probably not, due to the nature of his ambivalence, which strikes me as being slightly more positive than negative.

So, based on *that,* and based on my *years* of experience at estimating my prospects' varying levels of certainty, if I had to choose one number, I would place Bill at a 6, as opposed to a 5, although either choice won't affect the outcome.

Now, I just gave you a purposely verbose explanation to drive home a very important point—namely, that looping is as much an art as it is a science, so there's no need to make yourself crazy trying to figure out your prospect's exact level of certainty based on his response.

As long as you can discern his *approximate* level of certainty, then you have enough information to determine if you can safely move forward towards the close, or if you need to loop back to the front half of the sale to increase your prospect's level of certainty.

So, that being said, given the fact that I pegged Bill's response at a 6 on the certainty scale, does it make sense for you to move forward on the Straight Line towards the close?

The answer is *no,* absolutely not.

A 6 is not nearly high enough on the certainty scale for Bill or, for that matter, any of your prospects to seriously consider parting with their hard-earned money to buy something; and that's true whether they're buying $300,000 of Microsoft stock or *$500* of a penny stock; a $120,000 2017 Mercedes-Benz or a $500 ten-speed bicycle; a $90,000 state-of-the-art home theater system or a $399 forty-two-inch flat-screen TV; a $75,000 fast-food franchise or a $997 home-study course for the Straight Line System.

So, rather than moving forward and trying to close the deal, you're going to loop back to the front half of the sale instead—to the point on the Straight Line when you had just finished delivering the main body of your Straight Line sales presentation—and make a follow-up presentation that builds on the airtight logical case that you framed during your initial presentation.

In essence, your follow-up presentation picks up right where your logical frame left off—using your most powerful benefits and coherent assertions to turn the frame into an irrefutable, inarguable, scream-from-the-hilltops airtight logical case, while you use the advanced tonality technique of *pace, pace, lead* to start building emotional certainty as well.

With this one particular pattern, you're going to accomplish two crucial outcomes simultaneously: first, you're looking to increase your prospect's level of *logical* certainty to as close to a 10 as possible; and second, you're looking to begin the process of increasing your prospect's level of *emotional* certainty to as close to a 10 as possible.

Let's go through these processes step by step, starting with Bill's response, which landed him at a 6 on the logical certainty scale due to its ambivalent tone.

Specifically, Bill said, *"Yeah, it sounds pretty good."*

To that, your standard Straight Line response will be:

"*Exactly*—it really *is* a great buy down here! In fact, one of the *true* beauties here is . . ." and then you'll go directly into the main body of your follow-up presentation.

Similarly, if your prospect had said, "I guess so. It sounds okay," in the sort of dismissive tone that would have placed him at a 4 on the certainty scale, then you would say, *"Exactly*—it really *is* a great buy down here! In fact, one of the *true* beauties here is . . ."

And, once again, if he'd said, "Absolutely! It sounds like a great investment," in the sort of enthusiastic tone that would have placed him at an 8 or even a 9 on the certainty scale, then you would say,

"*Exactly*—it really *is* a great buy down at this level! In fact, one of the *true* beauties here is . . ."

In essence, just like the process of deflection, no matter how your prospect answers, and no matter where that answer lands him on the certainty scale, you're always going to respond with the exact same words; what's going to *change*, however, is your tonality.

Let me quickly explain.

Remember the story I told you about my son, Carter, being upset after soccer practice, and how I was able to quickly calm him down by using the tonal strategy of pace, pace, lead?

Well, that's exactly what you're going to do now—starting with the strategy's first step, which is to enter your prospect's world where he is, and then you'll pace him, and you'll pace him, and then you'll lead him in the direction that you want him to go.

For example, since the tonality in Bill's answer was at a 6 on the certainty scale, you wouldn't reply to him at a 10. (If you did, you'd instantly break rapport and be viewed as a high-pressure salesman.) Rather, you would reply at a level just above a 6—like a 6.2 or a 6.3—so that you're nudging him *ever so slightly* in the direction you want him to go, but you're still entering his world where he is. From there, you're going to transition into the main body of your follow-up presentation, where you're going to pace him, and then pace him, and then you're going to lead him in the direction that you want him to go by slowly increasing the level of certainty in your tone—timing it so that you hit your peak tonality about halfway through the pattern; then you'll maintain that tonality of absolute certainty straight to the end.

The one exception to this is if your prospect's response is below a 3 on the certainty scale. In that case, you're going to end the encounter right then and there and move on to the next prospect. After all, a prospect who still feels that negative about your product after you just completed framing your airtight logical case is not a real buyer. In fact, you're probably dealing with either a lookie-loo or someone with a warped sense of humor, as that level of negativity should have *definitely* come out during the intelligence-gathering phase and would have been weeded out accordingly.

It's for that very reason that responses below a 3 are extremely rare at this point. For the most part, you're going to be dealing with responses that fall between a 5 and a 7, with approximately 10 percent landing on either side.

Now, remember, deciding where your prospect landed on the certainty scale is not an exact science, so you need to use your common sense here. For example, if you've pegged your prospect at a 2 on the certainty scale, but something in your gut tells you that he still might be a buyer, then you want to repeat his negative answer back to him in an incredulous tone, and then ask again if that's how he truly feels about your product. If he responds anywhere above a 5, then you can start moving forward, albeit warily, as the philosophy of not trying to turn nos into yeses will continue to apply throughout the entire back half of the sale, with anything less than a 3 being the cutoff.

Of course, on the *flip side,* for every response above that, you'll transition into your follow-up presentation, using the same proven language pattern every time.

You're going to say, *"Exactly!* It really *is* a great buy at this level! In fact, one of the *true* beauties here is . . ." and then you'll go directly into your follow-up presentation, which must be so utterly compelling that even the most skeptical of prospects will have no choice but to become logically certain after hearing it.

In all seriousness, I can't even *begin* to overestimate the importance of this language pattern. It needs to make perfect sense from every angle—mathematically, economically, logistically, the value proposition, the benefit stack, the pain resolution, the energy expenditure, along with your strategic use of maximizers and minimizers and justifiers and power words and comparisons and metaphors and trustworthy figures—and then be flawlessly delivered, using the strategy of pace, pace, lead to create emotional certainty as well.

To complete the pattern, you're going to check in with your prospect by asking the same leading question every time (maintaining your peak tonality, from pace, pace, lead), which will allow you to gauge the increase in certainty for the first Ten. You're going to ask:

"You see what I'm saying here, Bill? Do you like the idea?"

Since you've already weeded out the last of the negative responders, you'll always get at least *some* type of yes, at this point, even if your follow-up presentation was total crap. The *problem* with that, however, is that a basic yes is no longer good enough, because what you're actually doing right now, with this first loop, is you're picking the lock to Bill's buying strategy.

Like all prospects, Bill has five numbers in his buying combination; and like all combination locks, not only do you need to know what all five numbers are, but you also need to know what order they go in.

With human beings, the first number you need to crack is the first Ten; and in order to consider it cracked, you need to hear an *enthusiastic yes* from your prospect that measures at least an 8 on the certainty scale, although the closer you are to a 10, the more certain you'll be that you got the number right. However, getting your prospect to a 10 can be very difficult to do sometimes, as a true 10 represents a state of such absolute certainty that it approaches the level of a conviction, and convictions aren't born in an instant; they take time to form, and they require repeated exposure to the same idea without a competing message to contradict it.

In consequence, getting your prospect to a 10 on the certainty scale will partially depend on the product you're selling. For example, if you're selling something that's quite well-known, with an impeccable reputation—like an iPhone or a Mercedes S-Class or stock in Facebook or tech support from Microsoft or a first-class train ticket on the Orient Express or a head-to-toe checkup at the Mayo Clinic—then you have an excellent chance of getting your prospect to a 10. Conversely, if you're selling an unbranded product that no one has ever heard of before, then a 10 is going to be a bit pie-in-the-sky.

A 9, on the other hand, is almost always doable. In fact, with only a few exceptions, you can always get a prospect to a 9 on the certainty scale, which is more than sufficient to close 99 percent of the prospects you'll speak to. And as far as the remaining 1 percent go, you can actually close those prospects too, although I'll circle back to them in a few minutes when we get to the fourth number in the buying combination: the action threshold.

So, that being said, you ended your follow-up presentation by saying to Bill, in a very enthusiastic tone: "You see what I'm saying here, Bill? Do you like the idea?"

To that, thanks to the irrefutable, airtight logical case you created, along with your successful implementation of pace, pace, lead, Bill's response will be exactly what you expected (and what you can expect from most prospects, provided that the quality of your follow-up presentations continues to remain high, and you embed them with the strategy of pace, pace, lead). Bill will reply, in a very enthusiastic tone, "Absolutely! I love the idea! It makes total sense to me!" to which you'll reply, in the same tone as Bill: "Exactly! The stock really is a screaming buy down here." And, *just like that*, you've closed out your pattern—moving Bill both logically *and* emotionally, in one swift swoop.

Now, a quick question:

Given that you just raised Bill's level of logical certainty to at least a

9 and his emotional certainty to at least a 7, does it make sense for you to take a shot and ask for the order again? After all, if it turns out that Bill has a low action threshold, isn't there a shot that you could slide in *under the wire,* as the phrase goes, and close him?

The answer is no, absolutely not.

You see, while Bill's first Ten is probably high enough now for him to justify buying, at this point in the sale all that's going to do is make him shift his focus to the *second* of the Three Tens, which is you, the salesperson, insofar as that Bill must trust you and connect with you at a very high level before you have any chance of closing him. And while the rapport you've built will go some way towards creating that connection, there is simply no justification for Bill to trust you at even close to a level that would make him comfortable enough to buy, or at least there's no justification yet; you're going to have to create one.

For that, you're going to use two very powerful language patterns that work hand in hand with each other to quickly move a prospect's second Ten to a significantly higher level while setting you up for a seamless transition to the third Ten.

Let me take you through them one at a time—starting with Bill's response to your follow-up presentation, which landed him at a 9 on the certainty scale for the first Ten.

"Absolutely!" he exclaimed. "I love the idea! It makes total sense to me!"

"Exactly!" you shot back. "The stock really is a screaming buy down here!"

And, *just like that,* you've formally closed out the last pattern, which you'll now use as a launchpad for the new one—putting a slight pause between the two to de-emphasize your sudden shift in tonality, from absolute certainty to one of mystery and intrigue.

You see, you're about to ask Bill a very profound question, using the tonality of *mystery and intrigue* in a way that will cause Bill to hear the following unspoken words: "A *very* interesting question just popped into my mind, out of nowhere, so it's obviously totally unrelated to my last question, as well as to your answer about loving my product, so feel free to answer it as if I had asked it to you in a vacuum!"

Now, of course, none of that is true, so you would never say such a thing; but by simply implying that through tonality, it will reduce any suspicions that may be building up over all the questions you're asking, especially since they're about to get a lot more pointed, starting now:

"Exactly!" you shot back, finishing your last pattern. "The stock really is a screaming buy down here!" Then you pause for a brief instant and switch to your mystery and intrigue tonality, and you say, "Now, Bill, let me ask you another question." And now you switch to your money-aside tonality. "If I'd been your broker for the last three or four years, making you money on a consistent basis"—and now you switch to your *implied obviousness*—"then you probably wouldn't be saying, 'Let me think about it right now, [your first name].' You'd be saying, 'Pick me up a block of at least a *few* thousand shares.' " And then you switch to the reasonable man tone and you add, "Am I right?"

Now, what you'll find here is that at least 95 percent of your prospects will come totally clean with you at this point, saying something short and sweet, like: "Yeah, well, then I would" or "Obviously! I mean, who wouldn't then, right?" or "Yeah, that would be a whole different thing."

Whatever variation you ultimately hear, at the end of the day, they all boil down to the same reality—that your prospect has just admitted that trust, or a lack thereof, is now *the* cornerstone issue for him, not *a* cornerstone issue.

In other words, once your prospects openly admit that they *love* your product, it significantly increases the importance of them openly admitting that it's *trust* that's holding them back from buying; and, taking it one step further, once they *do* admit that—that it's actually a lack of trust that's holding them back, not that bogus objection they hit you with—you've now cut to the heart of what the Straight Line System is all about, which is: pushing aside all the stalls and smoke screens (that cause the average salesperson to plunge into a rapport-breaking death spiral) so you get to the heart of what's *really* holding your prospect back, which is either a lack of certainty for one of the Three Tens, an extremely high action threshold, or a very low pain threshold. That's it.

Now, for that annoying 5 percent of prospects who reject your hypothesis—that it's actually a lack of trust that's holding them back, not some bogus objection—you're going to come at them with everything you've got.

Obviously, that doesn't entail snapping at Bill, in an angry, pissed-off tone: "Wait a second, moron—it's time to stop screwing around . . ." Instead, your voice is going to take on an almost mocking tone, mixed with complete incredulity. You're basically calling him out on his bullshit in a way that will earn his respect. You're going to say:

"Wait a second, Bill: you mean to tell me that if I put you into Union Carbide at 7 and took you out at 32, and I put you into U.S. Steel at 16 and took you out at 41, and I put you into Facebook at 70 and took you out at 130, then you wouldn't be saying, 'Pick me up at least a *few* thousand shares of Microsoft right now, on the spot, come on'?"

And with that, Bill, along with the rest of the 5 percent, will all come clean, and respond in basically the exact same way as the other 95 percent—saying, "Yeah, well, in *that* case, I would." The only difference is that many of them will answer in a slightly defensive tone, as if it wasn't *their* fault for flip-flopping on their answer; it was your fault for flip-flopping on your question. It's as if their tonality is so much as saying, "Well, why didn't you ask me that in the first place?" But, of course, that's precisely what you did ask them; the problem is that they weren't expecting to be called out on their bullshit, so now they're trying to backpedal and save face.

Whatever the case, you're still in excellent shape right now, as their defensiveness will quickly dissipate when you begin the next pattern, and you're now in a perfect position to close the sale—starting with the fact that you've successfully reframed what the sale is actually about.

You see, while Bill's original objection was "Let me think about it," rather than acting like every other salesperson and asking him the dead-end question "So, tell me, Bill, precisely what do you need to think about?" you took control of the sale and started picking the lock on his buying strategy.

Your prospect, on the other hand, is completely taken aback, because you've come at him in an entirely different manner than he's used to—including answering his objections before they even came up. Case in point: his *real* objection is that he doesn't know you, and therefore has no basis for trusting you; yet somehow you were able to bring that to the surface in a very elegant way. All you have to do now is figure out a way to get around *that*, which means convincing someone who you've only known for five or six minutes, and who you may have never met in person, and who may live on the other side of the country or, for that matter, the world, to trust you at a reasonably high level in the next sixty seconds.

It seems like a rather daunting task, doesn't it?

Well, believe it or not, it's actually quite simple—thanks to the existence of an extremely powerful language pattern that takes its name from the only person who possesses an IQ of 65 yet has still managed to get himself invited to the White House on three separate occasions to accept various achievement awards—including one for engaging in Ping-Pong diplomacy with China.

If you haven't already guessed, the remarkable individual I'm talking about here is none other than that Ping-Pong-playing, cross-country-running, premature-ejaculating, Jenny-loving fool named Forrest Gump, whose six-year-old incarnation served as the inspiration for the very language pattern that proudly bears his name: the Forrest Gump pattern.

Now, I think it's safe to assume that, unless you've been living in North Korea for the last twenty years, you've seen the movie at least twice by now, and probably three times.

Either way, there's a scene at the beginning where young Forrest is waiting for the bus to arrive on his first day of school, and he's standing there in his little leg braces, staring off into space, as he typically does. Then, suddenly, the bus pulls up, and all at once the door opens and Forrest looks up at the bus driver, and she looks down at him, and he just stands there, like a deer frozen in headlights, and he doesn't get on the bus.

The bus driver, a gruff-looking woman with a cigarette dangling from her mouth, is apparently not aware of who she's dealing with yet, so she says, in a brusque tone: "Are you coming on?"

To which Forrest replies, "Momma said not to be taking rides from strangers."

As she begins to realize what she's dealing with, the bus driver softens her tone a bit and says, "Well, this is the bus to school."

But, alas, this doesn't solve Forrest's core problem—that the bus driver is a stranger—so he just stands there, looking up at the lady sitting behind the wheel, who's looking back down at him, not sure what to do.

Suddenly, a wonderful inspiration sweeps over Forrest, and he figures out a way to break the deadlock with the simplest of phrases. He says, "My name is Forrest; Forrest Gump."

Impressed by the simplicity of Forrest's solution, the bus driver offers him a warm smile, and she replies, "Well, my name's Dorothy, and I'm your bus driver."

To that, Forrest shoots back: "Well, I guess we're not strangers anymore." And, feeling totally comfortable, he now gets on the bus.

Now, that's obviously a very simple example, but that doesn't change the fact that it's incredibly profound. You see, as a species, this is how human beings are built. When we've reached the tipping point, we can go from complete and utter distrust to an extremely high level of trust in a matter of seconds; yet, if you were to analyze these extreme swings on either side, you'd find that the truth typically lies somewhere in the middle, especially in a sales setting.

For example, over the years, I've been in literally *thousands* of situations where a prospect who'd been skeptical at the beginning, to the point of being *hostile,* would be cooking me a five-course meal thirty minutes later, as they went about calling their friends and relatives to tell them how they'd just met the world's greatest mortgage broker and that their friends should refinance their homes through *me* too—despite the fact that I hadn't done anything yet that was even *close* to warranting that type of glowing endorsement.

But, again, that's how human beings are built, especially in a sales setting. When that trust pendulum starts to swing, it swings all the way. The key to get it swinging is to take the time to write out a powerful Forrest Gump pattern *before* you enter the sales encounter.

So, let's go through that right now, picking up exactly where we left off—when Bill admitted that it was actually a lack of trust that's holding him back, not his original objection. And while his response was short and sweet— *"Yeah, well, in* that *case, I would"*—that doesn't take away from how profound it was. In fact, not only do those five simple words mark a major turning point in the sale but they also mark the point where you're going to begin your next pattern.

You're going to say, in a sympathetic tone: "Now, *that* I can understand. You don't know me, and I don't have the luxury of a track record; so let me take a moment to reintroduce myself.

"My name is [your first and last name], and I'm a [your title] at [the name of your company], and I've been there for [actual number] years, and I pride myself on . . ."

And now you're going to tell your prospect a little bit about yourself—citing any degrees you have, any licenses you have, any special talents you have, any awards you've won, what your goals are at the company, what you stand for as a person in terms of ethics and integrity and customer service, and how you can be an asset to him and his family over the long term.

In addition, in the same way that you took as much time as you needed to write out the best possible version of yourself, you also wrote out a secondary and a tertiary version as well. This will ensure that you can keep talking about yourself intelligently if the sale drags on, forcing you to execute additional loops.

So, you've now resold your product, which is the *first* of the Three Tens; you've resold yourself, which is the *second* of the Three Tens; and now it's time to resell the company that stands *behind* your product, which is the *third* of the Three Tens. And the way you're going to do that is by moving directly from the Forrest Gump pattern to a new pattern that has been designed to do precisely that—namely, to increase your prospect's level of certainty for the third Ten.

In other words, when you reach the end of the Forrest Gump pattern, rather than asking your prospect a question (like you've done with your previous patterns), you're going to move straight into your new pattern for reselling the company—using the following seven words as your transition: "And as far as my company goes . . ."

For example, let's say that the last point you were trying to get across to Bill with your Forrest Gump pattern was that not only are you going to tell him when to buy but you're also going to tell him when to sell. Here's how you would tack on your seven-word transition to the end of your Forrest Gump pattern. You would say:

"Not only am I going to guide you into the idea, but I'm going to guide you out as well. *And as far as my company, XYZ Securities, goes,* it's one of the most well respected . . ."

In essence, it's a seamless transition, where you're reselling the third Ten directly on the heels of reselling the second Ten.

Now, in order to create a kick-ass language pattern for your third Ten, you should follow the same protocol that I just laid out for creating your Forrest Gump pattern—including spending as much time as it takes to write out the best possible version of your company, on both a logical and an emotional basis; and, to be safe, I want you to create secondary and tertiary versions as well—ensuring that you can run additional loops without running out of intelligent things to say.

In terms of the specifics, you're going to be saying things like: "We're the number-one this . . . we're the fastest-growing that . . . we're the foremost experts in this . . . The chairman of the board, a man named so-and-so, is one of the most astute minds in the entire XYZ industry . . . He's accomplished X . . . he's accomplished Y . . . and he's built this company around one thing above all: [whatever that is]." And then you're going to complete this pattern by moving directly into a close, saying something along the lines of: "So, Bill, why don't we do this . . ." or "So, all I'm asking for is this . . ." and then transitioning directly into your close, which will end with you asking for the order a *second* time.

In addition, if the nature of your product allows it, one thing you should definitely consider here is to try to step down to a slightly smaller purchase, as it will definitely increase your conversion rate. In essence, you're allowing your prospect to "dip their toe in the water to test things out," and then, next time, after they've seen what a great job you've done, you can work on a much bigger level.

Here are a few quick examples of language patterns that work very well with this type of step-down approach:

- **"If you give me 1 percent of your trust, I'll earn the other 99 percent."**

- **"Frankly, on such a small sale like this, after I split my commission with the firm and the government, I can't put puppy chow in my dog's bowl."**

- **"I'm obviously not getting rich here, but, again, this will serve as a benchmark for future business."**

Now, to be clear, even if you're selling a product that *doesn't* allow for a step-down, that doesn't change the fact that this is the point on the Straight Line where many of your prospects will start to buy—especially the ones who have low action thresholds—as cracking the first three numbers of their buying combination is usually enough to close the deal.

On average, approximately 20 percent of the prospects who hit you with an initial objection will close right here, as a result of one simple loop. The rest of them, however, are going to require a bit more persuading, in the form of running additional loops that address one of the following three areas:

1 Increasing their level of certainty for one or more of the Three Tens

2 Lowering their action threshold

3 Increasing their pain threshold

RUNNING YOUR SECOND AND THIRD LOOPS

Congratulations!

You have reached the point in the sale where you're going to get to experience the distinct displeasure of objection hopping. For example, those prospects who had originally wanted to think about it will suddenly need to speak to their wives or their accountants, or they'll ask you to send them some information or they'll tell you that it's a bad time of year.

Now, for the vast majority of salespeople, getting hit with even *one* objection is enough to send the sale plunging into a death spiral. However, when they get hit with a *second* objection—which, like the *first* one, is nothing more than a smoke screen for uncertainty—that's when things start to get comical.

You see, when they get hit with the first objection, a typical salesperson will respond with a canned rebuttal—one specifically designed to overcome that objection—and then they'll ask for the order again. Of course, the problem with that is, unbeknownst to the salesperson, they just gave an answer that was designed to overcome a real objection, not a smoke screen for uncertainty about one of the Three Tens. In consequence, the salesperson's rebuttal won't exert even the slightest bit of influence over the prospect.

So, what does the prospect do?

Do they come clean with their respective salesperson and say, "Listen, pal, you might as well know that these objections I'm hitting you with aren't actually real; they're just smoke screens for uncertainty. I just thought that it was more respectful to say, 'Let me think about it,' than to say, 'I don't trust you,' which is what's *really* holding me back. It's nothing personal, by the way; it's only that you and I *just* met, so it's natural for me to feel this way.

"Besides, the truth is that I'm not 100 percent sure about your product, either. I mean, it *sounds* pretty good, but I *definitely* need to find out more before I buy."

Obviously, it would be extremely productive if your prospect came clean like that. Then you could start focusing on what actually matters, which is raising their level of certainty for the Three Tens and, if necessary, lowering their action threshold and then adding on pain. Unfortunately, though, that's not how things typically play out.

Instead of coming clean, the prospect takes the path of least resistance and switches to *another* objection, one that their salesperson hasn't had the chance to refute yet.

So, what does the salesperson do?

Like a dog chasing his own tail, the salesperson goes back to the list of canned rebuttals and chooses the one that's been designed to combat this new objection, and then repeats the process again—trying to sound as smooth and natural as possible—and then immediately transitions into asking for the order again.

Then the salesperson shuts up and waits for the prospect to answer—confident in the fact that, since they hit the nail right on the head with their latest rebuttal, the prospect should definitely say yes this time. But, of course, that's not what ends up happening.

Since the prospect has just gotten an answer to another objection that they couldn't care less about, they simply switch to yet *another* new objection, to which the salesperson then spits out yet another canned response, and on and on the death spiral goes.

You think I'm exaggerating?

Well, as unlikely as it seems, I'm not.

This is what happens, *all over the world*, when salespeople get hit with that first objection—unless, of course, they were lucky enough to have been taught the strategy of looping, in which case they sidestep the first objection using the strategy of deflection.

However, in the case of the second objection, you're going to have no choice but to address it head-on, as it would seem too evasive to keep deflecting objection after objection. The important thing to remember is that, whatever rebuttal you use to respond to your prospect's objection, all the answer does is give you the right to speak more.

Let me give you an example.

Let's say that Bill didn't buy after your first loop. Instead, when you asked for the order the second time, he said, "It sounds really good. Why don't you give me your phone number, and I'll call you back in a few days and let you know."

Your actual rebuttal to that objection would sound something like this:

"I hear what you're saying, Bill, but let me just say that I've been doing this for quite some time now, and if there's one thing I've learned it's that when people say they're going to think about it, or call you back, what ends up happening is that they end up putting the idea in the back of their mind and deciding against it, *not* because they don't *like* the idea—in fact, in your case I know that you actually do—but the simple fact is that we're both very busy people, and you'll go back to your busy life and end up missing out on this; and I don't want to see that happen to you.

"In fact, let me say this: one of the true beauties of the situation is that, right now, Microsoft is on the very cusp of . . ." And, *just like that,* you've seamlessly transitioned back into the sale, where you'll pick up right where you left off with building your airtight logical and airtight emotional cases at the end of your first loop.

In other words, when your prospect hits you with the second objection, you're not going to just *answer* it and ask for the order again; instead, you're going to *loop back* into the sale once more and move your prospect to an even higher level of certainty for each of the Three

Tens, using the secondary language patterns that you created for this exact purpose.

Now, from here, rather than going straight to the close (like you did with your first loop), you're first going to run an extremely powerful language pattern that will allow you to crack the *fourth* number in your prospect's buying combination—namely, their **action threshold**.

THE ACTION THRESHOLD

By way of definition, the action threshold is the collective level of certainty that a person needs to be at before they feel comfortable enough to buy. For example, I, personally, have a very low action threshold, which means that I'm extremely easy to sell to.

Why?

Because you don't have to *get* me to a 10, 10, 10 on the certainty scale to get me to buy. If you get me to a 7, 8, 7, that will probably be enough, especially if the purchase is going to resolve a pain that I'm feeling from an unfulfilled need.

Here's a perfect example:

A few years back, I was walking through an airport in Perth, Western Australia, and as I approached the gate I heard a loud *thwack* in the background, which sounded like someone had just hit the living hell out of a golf ball.

Sure enough, when I turned towards the sound, I saw a slender young Asian kid with a golf club in his hand, in a perfect trophy pose—as if he'd just finished hitting a three-hundred-yard drive straight down the middle. The kid was standing inside some type of promotional stand that had been roped off, and as I continued towards my gate, I watched him tee up another golf ball on an indoor mat and take a smooth, elegant swing. From where I was standing, it looked like he'd hit the ball straight through a window, although on closer inspection I saw that the ball was stuck to the face of the club.

As it turned out, some company had come up with a "revolutionary" golf training system in which they put Velcro on the face of a golf club and on a regulation-sized golf ball that was made of some sort of sponge-like material, so when you took a swing at the ball, it would stick to the face of the club; and, based on where it stuck, you could tell whether you were going to hit a hook or a slice.

In any event, I watched the kid take a few more swings, at which point I moseyed on over to take a closer look, and to get an explanation as to how the thing actually worked.

"It's really simple," he said confidently. "Watch, I'll show you!" And with that, he put the ball on a white plastic tee, and then he took his stance and proceeded to take a beautiful cut at the golf ball, one that would have easily sent it three hundred yards down the center of the fairway. However, when he showed me the head of the club, sure enough, there was the ball, stuck to the face of the club, as if it had been glued there.

"Look," he said proudly. "I hit this right on the inside of the ball—right here—so that would've been a nice, solid draw, about two hundred eighty yards in the short grass!" Then he went on to explain how you could also see if you were hitting the ball too close to the heel or toe, which would help you get rid of the most dreaded of all swing results: the *shanks*.

So, I took a few moments to consider everything—realizing the obvious fact that, what with golf being the hardest sport in the world to master, there was a very slim chance that this little contraption could improve my golf swing even one iota. Nonetheless, the sucker in me came shining through, and I asked, "How much does it cost?"

"It's only forty-nine dollars," he replied. "And it comes right in the box. You can carry it on the plane with you."

"Fine, I'll take it," I muttered, and, *just like that,* I bought it right on the spot, knowing full well that there was virtually no chance it was going to work.

But why?

Why would I make a decision that seemed to fly directly in the face of my own self-interest? The answer lies with the inner mechanics of how human beings, as a species, go about making their buying decisions.

Specifically, they run parallel movies through their minds.

In other words, the instant before you make a buying decision, your brain runs not one but two separate movies: it runs a positive one, which represents the upside potential, in the form of all the wonderful benefits that you'll get to experience in the future if the product turns out to be as awesome as the salesman has cracked it up to be; and it runs a negative one, which represents the downside risk, in the form of the all painful things that you'll experience in the future if it turns out that the salesman misled you, and the product is a total piece of crap. In other words, what's your best-case scenario, and what's your worst-case scenario?

Your brain runs both of these movies through your mind simultaneously, but it happens so fast that you don't even realize it. For example, with the golf training system, let's say the salesman had turned out to be a total scam artist, and his product was useless.

What's the worst thing that could have happened to me if I bought it?

Is a purchase of $49 going to put me in the poorhouse?

No, of course not!

Is it going to make my golf swing even worse?

I highly doubt it.

Am I going to feel like an idiot for getting taken to the cleaners?

No, again, because I spent only $49 on the thing. So what's the big deal?

And that's about as negative as I'll go, in terms of future pacing my downside risk.

However, when it comes to considering the upside potential . . . well . . . in *that* case, I'll *really* let my imagination go.

I'll be saying to myself, "Well, if this thing can help me get rid of those dastardly shanks I've been hitting and help me hit a beautiful drive like that skinny little Asian kid, then I can only imagine how great I'm going to feel when I'm sitting in the clubhouse with my buddies after a long round of golf, and we're having a few beers while I'm talking about my new and improved golf swing!"

Now, that's a perfect example of how someone like myself, with a *very low* action threshold, will play out a very empowering, positive movie, without any prompting from an outside force. And while I'll always make it a point to play out the negative movie too, I won't spend a lot of time doing it. Instead, I'll blunt that movie, both in length and intensity, turning it into a shorter and more watered-down version than it probably should be.

On the flip side of the question, let's look at someone who's literally the polar opposite of me—meaning, someone with an ultra-high action threshold, like my father, Max, who is literally one of the toughest buyers on the planet.

In point of fact, my father will not buy *anything* unless he is absolutely certain about all three Tens, and that means damn sure of them. There are no miracle golf cures getting sold to *him* in an airport. In fact, the moment he realized that the kid swinging the golf club was actually selling something, he would be like: "Who the hell does that kid think he is, selling some miracle golf cure? I mean, can't a man walk through an airport anymore without someone trying to sell him something?

Besides, what makes this kid an authority on golf? What a set of balls on this kid! What—a—set—of—balls!"

In consequence, if you get someone like my father to an 8, 8, 8 on the certainty scale, then there's simply no possible way they'll buy. Similarly, they won't buy at an 8, 10, 8 or an 8, 9, 8. The only way they'll buy is when you get them to a 10, 10, 10 and they're damn sure of it.

This is why we often find ourselves in situations where we're trying to close someone whose responses indicate that they're in a state of absolutely certainty (for all three of the Three Tens), yet we still can't get them over the line. Instead, they keep hopping from objection to objection, saying things like: "Let me think about it" or "Let me call you back" or "Send me some information," and so on.

So, what do you do in those cases?

The answer is, you lower your prospect's action threshold, right on the spot.

In total, there are four ways to do this.

The **first** way is to offer your prospect a money-back guarantee. This is a very simple, very common strategy that's used in countless different industries. It's especially prevalent on the Internet, where the chance of not getting what you *thought* you were paying for is significantly higher than in the offline marketplace, due to the presence of a large number of overseas vendors and unlicensed resellers.

The **second** way is to offer your prospect a cooling off or rescission period. This is a contractual feature that allows a prospect to make a binding decision now, but then reverse that decision for up to five business days. This is common in certain regulated industries, like real estate and vacation sales. While rescission periods are typically mandated by either a state or federal regulatory agency, that doesn't change the fact that they can still be used as a very powerful closing tool.

The **third** way is to use certain key phrases that paint a picture that runs counter to the worries and concerns that a typical high–action-threshold prospect ruminates on. Some examples of this are: "I'll hold your hand every step of the way" . . . "We pride ourselves on long-term relationships" . . . "We have blue-chip customer service."

And the **fourth**, and most *effective* way by far, is to use a very powerful language pattern that allows you to temporarily "reverse" a high–action-threshold prospect's parallel movies—causing them to abandon their strategy of running an unrealistically long negative movie and an extremely abbreviated positive one.

In other words, at the end of the day, the difference between my father and me is that, as a low–action-threshold person, my beliefs are such that when I'm faced with making a buying decision, I'll run a very long and very empowering positive movie, and a very short and not very toxic negative one. Conversely, as a very high–action-threshold person, my father's beliefs are such that, when *he's* faced with making a buying decision, he'll run a very long and very toxic negative movie, and a very short and very uninspiring positive one.

The way you go about reversing these movies is by using the aforementioned language pattern to *rewrite* their respective scripts along the lines of a low-action-threshold individual.

Here is an example of what you would say to Bill, if he were still sitting on the fence as a result of having an extremely high action threshold:

"Bill, let me ask you an honest question: what's the worst that can possibly happen here? I mean, let's say I'm wrong and the stock actually goes down a few points, and you lose two thousand bucks. Is that gonna put you in the poorhouse?"

"No," Bill replies a bit grudgingly.

"Exactly," you continue. "Of course it won't! And, on the upside, let's say I'm right—like we both think I am—and the stock goes up fifteen or twenty points, like we both think it will, and you make fifteen or twenty grand. I mean, it'll feel good and everything, but it's not gonna make you the richest man in town, now will it?"

"No, definitely not," replies Bill.

"Exactly! Of *course* it won't. It's not gonna make you rich, and it's not gonna make you poor, but what this trade *will* do is serve as a benchmark for future business. It'll show you that I can put you into the market at the right time, and take you out as well. So why don't we do this:

"Since this is our first time working together, why don't we start off a bit smaller this time. Instead of picking up a block of ten thousand shares, let's pick up a block of a thousand shares, which is now a cash outlay of only thirty thousand dollars. Of course, you'll make a bit less money as the stock trades higher, but your *percentage* gain remains the same, and you can judge me on that alone; and *believe* me, Bill, if you do even *half* as well as the rest of my clients in this program, the only problem you're going to have is that you didn't buy more. Sound fair enough?" And then you shut up and wait for a response.

In other words, if the prospect doesn't quickly answer, don't feel compelled to fill the conversational vacuum and start jabbering away and talking through your close.

You're at that magic moment now, when, in perfect sequence, you've summed up the very best benefits, you've reduced the energy expenditure, you've lowered the action threshold, and you've asked for the order in just the right way, using your tri-tonal closing pattern.

So, be quiet and let the client answer!

If you do, you'll find that about 75 percent of all the prospects who ultimately buy from you will do so right here. In essence, by taking these high–action-threshold buyers and, for a few fleeting minutes, lowering their action thresholds, you can then step through that window and close what are about to become your most loyal customers.

Indeed, if there's one thing about high–action-threshold prospects that makes them *more* than worth the extra effort it takes to close them, it's that they make excellent long-term clients. They're typically great tippers, they don't mind paying top dollar, and they almost never leave you for another salesperson, even if they get offered a better deal. They're basically *so* happy to have finally found a salesperson who was able to break through their limited beliefs and earn their trust that they'll stay put under almost any circumstance.

My father was a perfect example of this.

Growing up, I watched with fascination as he dealt with the same few salespeople to fill virtually all his needs, and he never questioned them about anything—about price, delivery times, competing products, the options or features they recommended, how much of a particular item he should buy, and what warranties he should take out. The bottom line is that he viewed each one of them as an expert in their respective fields, and he trusted their judgment on every level.

Ironically, it's these ultra-loyal, highly lucrative, high–action-threshold prospects, like my father, who end up slipping through the fingers of virtually all salespeople other than natural-born closers and those who have studied the Straight Line System.

To them, these otherwise "ultra-tough prospects" are nothing more than routine closes that had to be taken a *little* bit farther down the Straight Line as a result of their beliefs, which required the salesperson to crack the fourth number of their buying code—lowering their action threshold.

RUNNING ADDITIONAL LOOPS

So here we are, two loops down and . . . how many to go?

It's a good question, isn't it?

I mean, how many loops should you actually run?

Three loops? Four loops? Five loops? Ten loops? Twenty loops?

Before I fully answer that, let me start by saying that for those prospects who haven't bought yet, you're definitely going to run at least one more loop. After all, you still have one number left to address in their buying combination—namely, their **pain threshold**.

In essence, people who are feeling significant pain tend to act quickly; conversely, people who are in denial of their pain tend to act slowly. In consequence, there's actually an inverse relationship between the amount of pain a prospect is feeling and their action threshold.

In other words, in the same way that we can lower a prospect's action threshold by running a language pattern, there are also natural, everyday occurrences that can impact it as well; and when it comes to lowering the action threshold, the primary occurrence is how much pain they're currently feeling.

Here's a perfect example of how this plays out in real life:

When I was nine years old, my dad was driving us down to Washington, DC, in the family car as part of a two-week summer vacation that was going to take us all the way down to Miami Beach, Florida. We were somewhere around Delaware, about two hours from home, when the water pump blew out, and, all at once, the car started rattling and the lights on the dashboard were flashing and there was smoke coming from under the hood, and my father was muttering curses under his breath as he pulled over to the side of the road.

Now, what you need to understand here is that my father was extremely particular when it came to who could touch *any* of his possessions—and that includes basic, everyday items like his shirts, his ties, his wristwatch, his camera, and the very hair on his own head, which has been cut by the same barber for the last thirty years. But of all his possessions, the one he was most particular about, by far, was his car. Nobody—and I mean *nobody*—was allowed under the hood of my father's car except for one very special man: Jimmy at the local Sunoco station. Anyone else was strictly off-limits.

However, on that particular day, with his family stuck on the side of the road, 120 miles from home, with the sun going down and the temperature dropping, what do you think my father did? The answer is he went to the nearest gas station he could find and said to the owner: "I don't care what it costs. I need you to fix my car right now!"

The bottom line is that, at that very moment, the pain he was experiencing from the possibility of his family being in danger caused his action threshold to drop straight through the floor, and, *just like that*, he was transformed into one of the easiest buyers in the world.

This is why you introduce pain in two spots: first, during the intelligence-gathering phase, you want to identify where your prospect's pain lies and, if necessary, amplify it to ensure that your prospect listens to your presentation from that perspective; and second, you're going to reintroduce that pain right now, at the beginning of your third loop, using a language pattern that sounds something like this:

"Now, Bill, I know you said before that you're worried about your retirement in terms of Social Security not . . ." and so forth, and then you're going to raise the level of pain by asking your prospect what they think is going to happen with the situation if they fail to take action to fix it.

Using an empathetic tone, you would say: "Bill, let me ask you a question. Given how things have been deteriorating over the last twelve months, where do you see yourself in a year from now? Or, even worse, five years from now? Are things going to be even more intense, in terms of all the sleepless nights and the worrying?" And make sure that you maintain a very sympathetic tone throughout the entire pattern.

If you do, nine times out of ten, your prospect will say something like: "At best, I'll be in the same spot I'm in right now, but it'll probably be a lot worse."

And that's your chance to say, in the *I care* and *I feel your pain* tonality: "I get it, Bill. I've been around the block a couple of thousand times now, and I know that these things typically don't resolve themselves unless *you* take serious action to resolve them.

"In fact, let me say this: one of the true beauties here is that . . . ," and now you're going to quickly resell the Three Tens, using a concise yet very powerful consolidation of the tertiary language patterns that you created for each of the Three Tens, which will focus almost *exclusively* on the emotional side of the equation—using the technique of future pacing to paint your prospect that all-important pain-free picture of the future, where he can actually see himself using your product and getting the exact benefits he was promised and feeling great as a result of that; and, from *there,* you're going to transition directly into a soft close and ask for the order again.

Remember, with the exception of your first loop, in which you deflected your prospect's initial objection, your loops are always going to start by answering whatever new objection your prospect hopped to, using one of the dozens of proven rebuttals in the accompanying online resource,* albeit with a tacit understating that, no matter how awesome a rebuttal might sound, the only thing it's going to do is earn you the right to speak more; it's what you say *after* the rebuttal that's going to persuade your prospect to close.

Now, at this point, if the prospect sticks to the same objection, then you should thank them and let them move on with their life. After all, you don't want to be a high-pressure salesman and keep running loop after loop after loop after loop.

---

* Go to www.jordanbelfort.com/rebuttal to read about proven rebuttals.

In terms of the maximum number of loops you can run, from a theoretical perspective, the number is infinite, but I strongly suggest that you don't push the envelope like that. The reality is that you'll know by your prospect's demeanor when it's time to move on. If they start getting edgy or they're laughing overtly because they feel pressured, then you've gone too far.

In fact, as soon as you sense that your prospect is feeling even the slightest bit pressured, you immediately want to pull back and say something along the lines of: "Jim, please don't misconstrue my enthusiasm for pressure; it's just that I know that this *truly* is a perfect fit for you . . . ," and now you have two options.

Option one is to use this as an opportunity to loop *back* into the sale, yet again, and give it one more shot—paying very close attention to your tonality and body language as well as the tonality and body language of your prospect. In your case, you want steer clear of any unconscious communication that speaks of either absolute certainty or bottled enthusiasm, and focus on utter sincerity and "I feel your pain." In the case of your prospect, you want to focus on both their conscious and unconscious communication, and if either one signals that they're feeling pressured or perturbed in the slightest way, then I would immediately transition to option number two.

Option two is to use this as an opportunity to get back into rapport with your prospect so you can end the encounter on a high note, while also setting up the possibility for a callback. In this case, you would say something like: "Jim, please don't misconstrue my enthusiasm for pressure; it's just that I know that this *truly* is a perfect fit for you." Then you'd change your tonality to one of utter sincerity, and add: "So, why don't we do this: let me email you the information you're looking for"—or whatever the prospect's last objection was—"and then give you a few days to look through everything and also to discuss it with your wife"—or whatever their secondary objection was; if there was none, then you'd just omit this—"and then we can speak again next week, after you've had a chance to really get your arms wrapped around everything. Sound good?" And, from there, you can decide whether you want to set it up so that you're supposed to call the prospect back or the prospect is supposed to call you back.

Which path you choose depends on too many factors for me to give you a definitive answer without knowing the specifics of your industry; but, if there were only one factor I could consider above all, it would be what percentage of your callbacks ultimately end up buying. If the percentage is very low, then for the sake of time management, I would leave the ball in their court and wait for a callback—thereby assuring that you only talk to prospects who are truly interested.

On the flip side, if the percentage of callbacks that ultimately turn into clients is very high, then I would keep the ball in your court and instigate the callback yourself.

Just one final point with this—and that's to never forget the ethical side of the equation, which is that you do not want to use pain to disempower people; you want to use it to *empower* people by helping them make good buying decisions, so they can have the things that they truly need.

FINAL THOUGHTS

WHEN IT COMES TO THE REAL-WORLD APPLICATION OF THE Straight Line System, the most common mistake salespeople make is that they tend to be far too rigid when it comes to modifying the system's core language patterns to fit seamlessly into their industry.

For example, the vast majority of the language patterns I've covered will be a perfect fit for salespeople in industries like insurance, financial services, education, solar products, vitamins, network marketing, and pretty much any product or service where the *salesperson* initiates the sales encounter.

However, if you're working in a retail store, selling TVs or clothing or sporting goods or computers or just about anything else, then, obviously, it's not going to make much sense to ask a prospect if the shirt he just tried on makes sense to him.

So, in cases like that, where the initial pattern doesn't fit very well, all you need to do is adapt it to your current situation. For example, if you worked selling TVs in an electronics store, then you could say to your prospect "So, what do you think? Is this what you're looking for? Is this up your alley?" as opposed to saying "Does this TV make sense to you?" which sounds totally ridiculous.

Remember, when I first *invented* the Straight Line System, it was designed for selling five-dollar stocks to the richest 1 percent of Americans by cold-calling them on the telephone. *Since* then, I've taught the system to millions of people, in just about every industry you can imagine, and with just a bit of *tweaking of the core language patterns*, the results they've achieved have been truly staggering.

The point I'm trying to make is that, when it comes to applying the Straight Line System to industries *outside* the one it was originally designed for, the key to success is to be as flexible as necessary while you're creating your core language patterns—using your common sense as your guiding light to make sure that everything fits.

The Straight Line System is an immensely powerful persuasion system that can literally change your life in a matter of days. I've seen it happen all over the world, in countless industries.

People who had never achieved anything even *close* to resembling success are suddenly achieving things that they themselves had never dreamed possible, and they're living a life that's far more empowered than in their wildest dreams.

It all starts by mastering the art of persuasion, using the Straight Line System, while maintaining a clear understanding that you will never sacrifice your ethics and integrity along the way. After all, success in the absence of ethics and integrity is not success at all.

I had to learn that the hard way, but you don't—especially with this book as your guide.

APPENDIX

SYNTAX OF THE STRAIGHT LINE

- First four seconds

- Build and get into massive rapport, both conscious and unconscious

- Gather intelligence

- Transition to the body of the presentation

- Ask for the order

- Deflect and build certainty through the process of looping

- Lower the action threshold

- Add on pain

- Close the deal

- Massive referrals

- Develop customers for life

TEN CORE TONALITIES

1 "I care," "I really want to know"

2 Declarative as a question

3   Mystery/Intrigue

4   Scarcity

5   Absolute certainty

6   Utter sincerity

7   Reasonable man

8   Money-aside

9   Obviousness

10 "I feel your pain"

ACKNOWLEDGMENTS

There are a few people who I feel I must thank. Obviously, my agent, Jan Miller, who is a true force of nature, and the whole editing team at Simon & Schuster. Their infinite patience with my glacial writing pace was above and beyond. Without them this book would probably still be in the draft phase. Thank you all for the sometimes-less-than-gentle nudges and basically forcing me to finish. I also want to thank my manager, Scott Lambert, who has always had faith in me, no matter what project we started on, and Alexandra Milchon, who first made me believe that I could really succeed as a writer. Without your unflagging support, I'm not sure that I would be where I am today.

I also want to send a special thank-you to my dear friend Barry Guesser. If he were here today, I know that he would be one of my greatest cheerleaders. His belief in me and his advice and support throughout the years will never be forgotten. I miss you, Barry.

To my family: Anne, Carter, Chandler and Bowen, I know this book has been all-consuming, so thank you for allowing me to put the time I needed to into this endeavor. I can't wait to be fully present for all of you again, in my own semi-present way that you all love to make fun of. Also, I need to give a quick shout-out to Jeff Turango, whose morning tennis sessions, where he never made a single unforced error, kept me sane during the weeks; and then Vince Spadea, whose morning tennis sessions kept me sane on the weekends, when I wasn't busy chasing after all the winners he hit or trying to figure out how someone could never stop talking while they played, yet still be one of the top players in the world.

Most importantly, though, I want to thank my parents for their unwavering support of me through all my life's twists and turns. They made all of this possible. I love you, Mom and Dad, and can't thank you enough.